RIVALS ACROSS THE RIVER
THE STORY OF HULL'S RUGBY LEAGUE DERBIES

RIVALS ACROSS THE RIVER
THE STORY OF HULL'S RUGBY LEAGUE DERBIES

BY DAVID BOND

First published in Great Britain byThe Breedon Books Publishing Company Limited
Breedon House, 44 Friar Gate, Derby, DE1 1DA. 1999

This paperback edition published in Great Britain in 2015 by DB Publishing, an imprint of JMD Media Ltd

ISBN 978-1-78091-464-0

Printed and bound in the UK by Copytech (UK) Ltd Peterborough

Contents

Sowing the Seed

SOMETIMES it can be decidedly convenient to be a Hull City supporter if you follow professional sport in East Yorkshire. You go through enough bad times to appreciate the good, but you can suffer those disappointments and setbacks as moments of private grief. You may share them with your fellow fans, but by and large the emotions can be kept in reasonable check.

One reason why it is a lot easier to digest defeat if you follow the Tigers is because the splendid isolation of the city of Hull – once memorably described as being 40 miles down a railway siding – dictates that you do not have to put yourself through the stress of local derby games in which much, much more is at stake. There is no great tradition lurking savagely in the foreground because the other clubs nearest to Hull have never produced the deadly rivalry that might naturally exist elsewhere.

It is, however, a very different story in professional rugby league circles in Hull because you do not have to look very far for traditional derby clashes – just across the banks of the River Hull, in fact, as it wends its weary way northwards through the heart of the city from its confluence with the River Humber. Hull has produced two notable professional rugby league clubs – known locally for most of their existence as Hull FC and Hull Kingston Rovers – and they have set up their respective encampments across the river from each other. Hull have traditionally been to the west of the divide with Rovers to the east of it. It is immensely ironic, therefore, to contemplate that in the early days of rugby in the city it was the opposite way round.

Hull are the senior club and have an uninterrupted history dating back to 1865 when they were formed by a group of ex-public schoolboys from York. They joined the Rugby Union in 1872 and were peripatetic in the early days, using grounds at Woodgates Hall in North Ferriby; opposite the Londesborough Arms in Selby; at Hull Rifle Barracks' field in the city's Londesborough Street; at the Haworth Arms field in North Hull; and at West Park near the present base. But in 1881 they amalgamated with White Star, whose 5,000-capacity, 12-acre ground at Hall's Field off Holderness Road in East Hull they used.

Rovers, on the other hand, were formed as Kingston Amateurs by a group of apprentice boilermakers in 1883 and their first ground was at Gillett Street off Hessle Road in West Hull. It was so cramped that a set of flagstones formed one touchline and it became known as 'Flag-Edge Touch'. And Kingston Amateurs became just as itinerant as their local rivals. They switched to a field off Anlaby Road in West Hull, changed their name to Hull Kingston Rovers when they moved the short distance to Chalk Lane for the 1885-86 season and two years later switched to

Hessle Road Locomotive Ground when Dairycoates was an outlying village to the west of Hull. A further move to a ground opposite the Star and Garter on Hessle Road followed before Rovers, already known as the Robins because of their red jerseys with a blue band, started to play on the Hull Athletic Ground off the Boulevard in West Hull in 1892.

When Rovers' lease at the Hull Athletic Ground expired three years later, they could not raise the capital to buy the land from the local railway company who owned it. But their older and wealthier neighbours Hull stepped in, crossed the river from Hall's Field, which was on the site of the present Mersey Street and Severn Street, and have been on the west side of the city ever since, playing their first game at what became known as the Boulevard against Liversedge on September 21, 1895. The ground is situated in Airlie Street, so it was obvious and convenient for Hull to be nicknamed the Airlie Birds.

And while Hull were moving to the west, Rovers crossed the river to the east, where they have remained ever since apart from one cup-tie at the Boulevard in 1898 and a few home derbies in West Hull at Boothferry Park between 1953 and 1959. Initially the Robins settled at the Craven Street Ground which had previously been the home of the old Southcoates club and they soon amalgamated with the Albany soccer club under the guise of Hull Town Association Club. It was not long, though, before the soccer club moved west to Dairycoates and became Hull City.

But soon after World War One, Rovers became restless again and sites for a new ground at Barnsley Street, which was not far from the old Hall's Field, and next to the Four Halls Hotel became possibilities. In the end the club decided to develop a site near the tram and bus depot towards the eastern end of Holderness Road and moved from Craven Street to Craven Park, where they played their first game against Wakefield Trinity on September 2, 1922. As World War Two broke out, Rovers were struggling, so they sold Craven Park to a greyhound syndicate, making it a dual-purpose sporting ground. They are still at Craven Park, of course, but it is a different ground with the same name. Various sites had been mooted for a possible switch in post-war years, but eventually they settled for a new rugby and greyhound stadium at the former Shakespeare Hall High School on Greatfield. They had moved a little further east and the first game at the new Craven Park took place against Trafford Borough on September 24, 1989.

But back in those early days when Hull moved from east to west, they were deemed to be unsportsmanlike for gazumping Rovers to take over at the Boulevard and it has always been accepted that both clubs lost some of their traditional support in the wake of their moves across the city. Bit by bit, though, an intense rivalry between rugby factions in the east and west was becoming entrenched and over the years it has expressed itself in some quirky ways.

Take the example of well-known local publican Jack Collins in the 1980s. A passionate Black-and-White who had worked hard for a number of years on Hull's behalf, he could hardly believe his misfortune when he was moved from the Providence Inn in the city centre – which was to the west of the river, of course – to a public-house in the opposition territory in East Hull. And someone in the brewery's higher echelons was obviously somewhere between a wicked sadist at worst and a mischievous humorist at best because they moved him to a place called the Robin!

But right from the early days there was only one way in which the rivalry between the opposing rugby camps could truly blossom – on the pitch. Early in 1999 Rovers caused a stir when they rejected an offer by Hull to play them in a derby and 100 years earlier there were times when there were obstacles to be overcome, but in the end they were not insurmountable.

Arrangements were finally made for the inaugural derby showdown between Hull and Rovers and that first meeting took place on Friday, September 16, 1899, at Craven Street. The gates were opened at 12.30pm and a band played on the field for two hours until the 3.30pm start. Boys were charged 3d., while the full entrance fee was three shillings and spectators were told: 'It must be distinctly understood that no change will be given and that no money will be returned.' As it was, 20 Rovers supporters were understood to have got into the ground the night before to sleep there!

Interest in the game was phenomenal and it was eagerly reported: 'Before 12 o'clock a crowd of about 100 people assembled at the entrance and many of them were armed with cards and sandwiches in order to wile away the weary hours. The crowd, like a rolling snowball,

gathered size and eventually became gigantic. Hull's fiery chariots deserted the main roads and collected in a long procession at the corner of Savile Street. The tingling of the hansom bell and the occasional presence of an imposing 'four-wheeler' lent the utmost animation to the cavalcade. It is well-known that, in consequence of improvements, the road to Craven Street is thoroughly disorganised, so the journey to the ground was to some extent like an obstacle race. At the end of Dock Street rulleys, wagonettes, cabs, perambulators and people were hopelessly mixed, while in George Street several vehicles 'cannoned' with a rather volcanic effect.

'The police officers were very courteous and did not take the names of any drivers for overcrowding. Every three yards along the road there was a policeman, while shortly after 12 o'clock 13 stalwart specimens mounted guard at the end of Craven Street. Consequently, law and order were upheld.

'Some people had an idea that many would stay away on account of the probability of a crush. But football fanatics are not built that way. Until three o'clock a steady stream of serious-faced, would-be spectators streamed into the east. There were no beaming countenances: the issue at stake was far too awful. All was 'measured tread' until the gates were reached and then it was first-come, first-through.

'The gentler sex, of course, were not represented, but Hull's juvenility turned out in myriads. There was also a hansom, into which six burly spectators had packed themselves. It was like a huge sardine tin on wheels. Many people dis-

Hull FC in 1901-02 soon after Hull rugby league derbies began.

played gaily-coloured shields in their hats with mottos exhorting Hull and Rovers 'to play up'. Despite the fact that East Hull contains more than three wise men, prophets were few and far between and betting ruled evens.'

That then was the backcloth to the first derby and it was duly completed by an argument between a 'Redbreast' and a 'Blackbird', but eventually the two fans apparently calmed down and agreed to 'exchange chews of tobacco'. The 15-a-side game, comprising just nine local players, began on time in front of an estimated 12,000 crowd with Rovers' Jack Rhodes getting the derby series under way when he kicked off towards the Craven Street end. And after a scramble in the first minute Anthony Starks pounced to become the first player to

score in a derby when he put Rovers ahead with a try. He missed the conversion – or 'place' in those days – with what was described as 'a miserable effort', but on the stroke of half-time the Robins increased their lead with a try by Albert Kemp, whose conversion struck the bar without going over. Hull, then known as the All-Blacks, reduced the arrears with their first derby points when Jacques dropped a goal to make it 6-2, but Rovers completed an 8-2 victory near the end when Tulloch fielded a punt from Cyril Lempriere and dropped a goal of his own.

The derby trend, therefore, had been set once and for all at a time when it was deemed that 'the rivalry of Roman gladiators and Spanish bull-fights are quite in the shade compared with the popular-

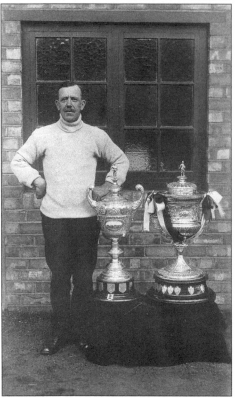

Billy Jacques, who scored Hull's first points in a derby in 1899.

the wake of the long-awaited practical evidence. At the time, the impact of that first derby clash was summed up as follows: 'Thousands of arguments and countless comparisons have been at one time or another addressed in favour of one team or the other, but, because the teams had not met, all the talk was purely conjectural and the most absurd of hypotheses might have been advanced on this score without fear of its being upset. But there will now be some grounds for the critics and debaters to work upon. And as long as the rugby code shall hold its sway in Hull, the 16th day of September, 1899, is a date that will be firmly impressed on the minds of local followers of the game. The first meeting of Hull and Kingston Rovers has been an event of no small moment and has been eagerly anticipated for a considerable period by all sections of the public. In course of time the fixture is bound to lose much of the charm of novelty – although the fact of the contending parties being close neighbours will always render it more than usually attractive – but the initial encounter was an attraction, the like of which has never before been known in the city.' Battle had indeed commenced.

ity of the rugby code in the country's third port'.

Previous attempts to arrange a derby clash had foundered: this time it had been full steam ahead and a lot of unsubstantiated opinions could finally either gain credibility or fall by the wayside in

Both Sides Now

RUGBY league fans in Hull have a habit of wanting the best all-round for their code because they believe in it so passionately and single-mindedly. There is a community spirit that does put the game itself on a pedestal, probably in the belief that it has never been a thoroughly national sport in England because it is too hard for so-called southern 'softies', and its followers are genuine, committed and loyal. They want the best for rugby league and they want more and more people to derive pleasure from it. In Hull, though, there is always one burning question asked of any fan: 'Are you Black-and-White or Red-and-White?' You are duty-bound to declare your allegiance to Hull FC or Hull Kingston Rovers. Only then can you reasonably discuss the ramifications of the game as a whole within the city's confines.

It means that once a fan declares his or her loyalty to either Hull or Rovers, then it is engraved in tablets of stone, in an ideal world it should have all the hallmarks of a sporting marriage made in heaven and it is certainly permanent and unchanging. No fan would then dream of the prospect of having a change of heart, undergoing some kind of mystical, magical transformation on the road to either the Boulevard or Craven Park and then going over to the other side. You made your oval bed with either Hull or Rovers and you laid on it for life. A Clintonesque impeachment would probably follow for anyone who dared otherwise.

It is, therefore, a source of wonder that although a fan could not change sides, a player certainly could. And plenty of them certainly did. Some of the greatest stars in Hull's rugby league firmament played for both clubs or had other connections, normally in a coaching capacity, with them both. Their double lives have fallen into various categories as circumstances dictated.

Billy Jacques set one trend by playing for Hull and then joining Rovers' backroom staff as their trainer. He played in the first two derbies for Hull, kicking a goal in the inaugural clash in 1899. There is probably a feeling, though, that if you changed loyalties as a result of playing or coaching opportunities, it was a more difficult step to take if you were originally from the city.

Johnny Whiteley was arguably one of the local all-time greats to try to bridge the gap. Known throughout rugby league as 'Gentleman John', he played local soccer for Fish Trades and was a noted swimmer while he was a PT instructor with the Military Police. He joined Hull after demobilisation from the Military Police in December 1950 even though several of his Hull Boys' Club colleagues had gone to Rovers. The simple fact was that although Rovers wanted him, he wanted to play only for Hull. Whiteley was the leader whose brother Peter played alongside him in the days of the Airlie Birds' 'great pack' and he became a Boulevard legend, taking over as captain from the late Mick Scott. He twice captained Great Britain after establishing himself as an international loose-forward and was appointed as the Airlie Birds' player-coach after Roy Francis moved to Leeds. A shoulder injury ended his playing career during the 1964-65 season and he signed a five-year contract as Hull's coach, but resigned in 1970. Colin Hutton, with whom he had playing and coaching links, then coaxed Whiteley across the river to coach the Robins, but they sacked him in 1972 and he resigned from his work with Great Britain soon afterwards. But during his coaching career Whiteley had also been the assistant manager of Great Britain's tourists, coached the Yorkshire representative side and become the first man to hold three top-level jobs by coaching Great Britain, England and Great Britain Under-24s. Whiteley later helped to set up top amateur side West Hull, ventured into clubland ownership, ran a successful gymnasium and might even be spotted just behind one of the manager's dug-outs watching Hull City's reserves in his own unassuming way.

But even though brothers Johnny and Peter Whiteley played alongside each other with Hull, there were still split family loyalties. Johnny Whiteley might have ended up having a brief spell as Rovers' coach, but he is naturally associated with the Airlie Birds. Yet his uncle, Jack Hoult, had played for the Robins. And he was related by marriage to John McIntyre and Billy Westerdale, who had also played for Rovers. In fact, there is a recurring theme – delightful or distressing, depending on how you look at it – of divided families created by those who were connected with both clubs.

And derby rivalry is steeped in the possibility of splitting family loyalties. Billy Batten, snr., was an early all-time great as a threequarter with Hull from April 1913 when he joined them from Hunslet for a £600 fee until he moved to Wakefield Trinity 11 years later before ending his playing career with Castleford. Born at Kinsley, near Pontefract, Batten, who died in Stanley Royal Hospital, Wakefield, in January 1959 at the age of 69, had three sons, Billy, jnr., Eric and Bob. Billy, jnr., joined Hull shortly before his father's career at the Boulevard ended, but moved to Rovers after two years. The other two sons steered clear of local rivalries in Hull because Eric was Batley's manager and played for Wakefield Trinity, Hunslet, Bradford Northern and Featherstone Rovers, while Bob played for Castleford.

Billy Teall, who was born in Hull in May 1912, was a product of the city's prolific Courtney Street School team and soon became acclimatised to a derby atmosphere because he played his first game for Hull A against Rovers A at Craven Park. A full-back, he made his first-team debut for the Airlie Birds in 1931, but spent much of his career with Wakefield Trinity. But he had spells with Hull KR and Keighley during World War Two and had a stint with Belle Vue Rangers, who had previously been the noted Broughton Rangers, after it. "During the war you could just about play for anybody and I had about half-a-dozen games for Rovers as a guest player," he said of his move across the river. It was by no means unknown and had happened on several occasions during World War One when guest players became available for both Hull clubs.

Teall, who also played for a Rugby League Select XIII against the Army at the Boulevard, was well aware of the intensity of local loyalties in his day. "Everybody was dead keen in derby games and they got a bit rough at times because it was glory if you won and that made it a lot better if you went out to a pub on the night-time after the game. It was always rough, but that was only because you played to win. And if you were playing for Hull, it was always a bit more special to go and beat Rovers at what was the old Craven Park", he said. Teall was well aware of divided family loyalties, though, because he was related by marriage to scrum-half Maurice Daddy, who played for Rovers from October 1945 to April 1953 before emigrating to New Zealand, where he died.

And there were plenty of other examples of families having their feet in both rugby league camps in Hull. In 1977 Hull signed half-back Peter Hall while his brother David, a Great Britain international, was with Rovers. Peter Hall had been released after three years with Rovers Colts. The Robins signed brothers David and Peter Walker, but one of their other brothers, Malcolm, played for the Airlie Birds. Hull signed forward Mick Sutton, whose father Tom had played for both city clubs. Mick Sutton's grandfather Tom had also played for Hull, but Tom Sutton, jnr., made his bow with Rovers after joining them from Hull

George Bateman, who made his derby debut for both Hull and Rovers on a Christmas Day.

Boys' Club in September 1951 and then popped up with the Airlie Birds in January 1959. Terry Major signed for Rovers as a 17-year-old in November 1959, but his uncle was Harold Ellerington, who made his name as a scrum-half and then loose-forward with the Airlie Birds. He later became a director of Hull at the time that Major was playing for Rovers.

But players with divided loyalties after being with Hull and Rovers might arguably have had more pangs of conscience if they were locals through and

Joe Oliver played for Hull in 20 consecutive derbies from Christmas Day 1929 to Christmas Day 1937. He then played in the next three for Rovers.

through, as in the case of Johnny Whiteley. Perhaps it was a little easier to switch loyalties across the river if you were an outsider in the first instance because you were never naturally associated with one side of the divide. You would soon know about the fans' passion on arriving in Hull, but you always had the possible get-out clause that the fierce rivalry was nothing really to do with you because you were in essence an outsider just looking in for the time being. And certainly some of the greatest players and coaches who have crossed the great divide have been outsiders and probably respected by the public on both sides of the river for what they did for rugby league itself above all.

One of the best examples of an outsider who was taken to the public's hearts on both sides of the River Hull was Clive Sullivan. A man of great dignity, he died tragically young in Hull's Kingston General Hospital at the age of 42 in October 1985, but it was not long afterwards that the main A63 trunk road into Hull was named after him – Clive Sullivan Way – as a mark of the universal esteem in which he was held in the city.

He was not the first player to emerge from Wales and play for both clubs. For example, Tom Danter, a prop forward, signed for Hull from Welsh rugby union club Bridgend in October 1948. A Welsh international, he moved to Dewsbury in January 1951 for £2,000, but he made one appearance for Rovers in a derby in 1956. Sullivan, though, made much more impact, stemming from the first time that he burst sensationally on to the rugby league scene in Hull as a mystery trialist. The Airlie Birds had just signed South African winger Wilf Rosenberg from Leeds for £5,750 and his debut against Bramley in December 1961 was awaited with much anticipation. Rosenberg twice crossed for tries on his first appearance, but he was upstaged by the trialist winger who touched down three times. It was Sullivan, who came originally from Cardiff – born in Splott and brought up in the famed Tiger Bay area – and had been serving in the Royal Corps of Signals. In the Army he had been a top-class sprinter, played some

Clive Sullivan, scorer of a record seven tries for Hull. The main A63 trunk road into Hull was named after him.

rugby union and done some boxing, he had also had rugby league trials with Bradford Northern when his unit was based at Catterick Garrison. He had then been transferred to the south, but Hull's coach Roy Francis traced him and offered him a trial. The rest is history – with its fair share of ups and downs. At one stage he was, for example, awarded the MBE and then lost the Great Britain captaincy 24 hours later. In addition, 'Sully' scored a record seven tries for Hull against Doncaster in 1968, he was capped by Great Britain and Wales, he was honoured on *This Is Your Life* and he had a stint as coach at the Boulevard. But he had some lengthy injury absences and there were times when he was unsettled with Hull. It all came to a head in a dispute about his testimonial in March 1974 when Hull accepted his resignation as coach, promoted David Doyle-Davidson in his place and slapped an £8,000 price tag on him. A month later he joined Rovers at the age of 31 in a £3,250 deal although he agonised about the switch of local allegiance. Sullivan stayed at Craven Park until 1981 and won a winner's medal at Wembley with the Robins in the all-Hull Rugby League Challenge Cup final of 1980. It was one major honour to have eluded him and he had had to cross the river to achieve it. He once asked Rovers for a transfer, too, before withdrawing his request and he had brief spells with Doncaster, where he was coach for 14 months from March 1983, and Oldham, but he did return to the Boulevard towards the end of his playing career.

He was associated with Sully's nightclub and was a building society manager:

above all, he was revered on both sides of the river and remains the only player to reach the 100-try mark with both Hull and Rovers. But even Sullivan could not escape from divided family loyalties because his brother Brian followed him to Hull in March 1962 and his son Anthony made his name with Rovers on his way to becoming a Great Britain international.

Another outsider to serve both Hull and Rovers successfully in different capacities was Colin Hutton. He was with his home-town club Widnes for four seasons before joining Hull in March 1951 and played mainly at full-back, becoming involved in some notable goalkicking dramas with contrasting results during a successful era based around the club's legendary 'great pack'. Towards the end of his playing career Hull had encouraged him to take up coaching and offered him the job as A-team coach, but it was not to be and he was transfer-listed. He was linked with Doncaster and York, but Rovers refused to meet Hull's asking price for him as a player even though it had been reduced from £1,500 to £1,000 and to £500, so Hutton signed a four-year deal purely as a coach in the wake of Joe Ramsden's resignation after 16 months in charge. 'Hull's attitude seemed to be that I could go anywhere but Rovers', he reflected of the local rivalry. It meant that he joined Rovers as their coach at the age of 31 in November 1957 and yet was still on Hull's register as a player – a classic case of divided loyalties, in theory at least! Hutton spent 13 years as Rovers' coach and then as their general manager when Johnny Whiteley was persuaded to cross

the river to succeed him as coach. In March 1974 Hutton, who also coached Great Britain and England, became a director at Craven Park, later becoming chairman as they embarked on a revival that heralded a special era in their history. And, as a publican, Hutton also crossed the river from west to east when he moved from the Avenue Hotel, a hostelry with strong rugby league links, to the Zetland Arms.

Another contemporary outsider who basically went in the opposite direction was Arthur Bunting, who had joined Bramley from junior rugby in Featherstone during the 1956-57 season. Colin Hutton brought him to Rovers in October 1959, paying Bramley a fee of £1,250, and Bunting was soon labelled 'the best uncapped scrum-half in Yorkshire'. It looked as if he were going to cross the river as a player in January 1968 when Rovers agreed on a £1,000 fee with their rivals, but then Hull decided not to pursue their interest after holding a board meeting. Bunting instead became the Robins' coach after Johnny Whiteley had been sacked in February 1972, moving up after a spell as A-team coach. But he left Rovers after a successful spell with them amid allegations of interference from a minority of his directors and he resigned as coach five days before they were due to meet Leeds in the Yorkshire Cup final at Headingley in November 1975. Bunting finally made it to the Boulevard in January 1978 when Hull appointed him as their new team manager following the resignation of coach David Doyle-Davidson. He nearly kept them in the First Division and was rewarded with a three-year contract, which was the springboard to immediate promotion and another successful era. Bunting stayed with Hull until December 1985 and has latterly run a residential home in the Holderness village of Ryehill.

Joe Oliver was an outsider from an earlier era and was born in Maryport in Cumberland. A goalkicking centre, he played for Huddersfield and Batley before joining Hull for £800 in October 1928 and rapidly established himself as one of their all-time heroes. The fans' catchphrase of the day was 'Give it to Joe' and he played for them in 20 consecutive derbies from Christmas Day 1929 to Christmas Day 1937. He then played in the next three derbies for Rovers, kicking two vital goals when they beat Hull 13-12 in the first of them on April 15, 1938, exactly a month after moving across the river. Oliver, who died in Hull Royal Infirmary at the age of 61 in June 1966, returned to Hull during World War Two and played until he was nearly 40. He then had spells as trainer-coach with both Rovers from July 1946 and then Hull for a year from July 1949. A driver in later life, he had upset Hull's fans with his initial pre-war move across the river as a player and there was briefly an outcry about it.

And it was another typical example of much of the thinking about transfers over the years – a player might move anywhere apart from to the opposition across the river. The problem was probably that selling directors were wary of any backlash from the fans and that influenced their manoeuvres irrespective of the value of the deal.

Such moves also beg the question as to whether the grass was ever greener on the other side of the river because some of the players who were on the books of both Hull and Rovers will often be inextricably linked with one club rather than the other. It also brings up the point as to whether it can always be the same when a player moved across the river after spending most of his career with the opposition.

Jim Drake, for example, will always be best remembered as a member of Hull's 'great pack' of the 1950s, but he and his contemporary forwards, Johnny

Johnny Whiteley, arguably one of the all-time local greats. He first joined Hull in 1950 after service in the Military Police.

Whiteley and Bob Coverdale, switched allegiance. And Drake, who packed down with his elder twin brother Bill at the Boulevard, caused a sensation in November 1961 when he signed for Rovers after being transfer-listed by Hull at £4,000. And he admitted: 'Roy Francis was a marvellous man at Hull and certainly the best coach of his era, but Harry Poole and Cyril Kellett were fantastic blokes to be with at Rovers. But I honestly don't think that the team spirit at Rovers was quite as good as it had been at Hull. I had some happy times with Rovers, but after 12 years with the pack we had at the Boulevard, it was probably never going to be the same'. The Drakes were also outsiders, originating from Cumberland, but coming through the ranks with top York side Heworth. Yet again, though, there were divided family loyalties – Jim Drake played for both clubs, his twin Bill was with Hull and another brother Joe joined Rovers.

The fans frequently frowned on moves across the river or on players who were with both Hull clubs even if there were a diplomatic lapse of time, probably involving an outside club, in-between. Such moves across the city were regarded as the ultimate in rugby league treachery by the public and their strong emotions were perfectly understandable, but a more objective outlook would be from the players' own standpoint. They were professionals and, as such, were keen to earn some kind of living from their chosen sport while they could and wherever they could. If that meant taking a trip across a river in Hull to achieve that purpose, so be it. It was convenient at any rate.

Tommy McGeiver, for example, was one of the first players to take advantage of playing for both clubs for geographical ease. His career started with his home-town club Widnes before he moved to Leigh and then to Rovers in 1913. Nine years later he joined Halifax, but soon became tired of commuting between East and West Yorkshire on his own, so he solved the problem by joining Hull, for whom he played for 18 months.

Bob Coverdale was with the Airlie Birds as their 'great pack' developed, but they transfer-listed him at £2,000 in January 1957.

The last pair of boots worn by Clive Sullivan with three of his awards – his MBE and Rugby League Challenge Cup winning medals. They had been prepared for an exhibition in Hull's old Grammar School museum.

McGeiver, a half-back, later worked on Hull Fish Dock until his retirement in 1959.

Stand-off half Rowley Moat, whose brother-in-law Terry Murray played soccer for Hull City and was a Republic of Ireland international, began his rugby league career with Hull before joining Oldham in a £2,000 deal. He had a brief, unhappy stay at Watersheddings and left Oldham to sign for Rovers from Oldham for £500 in December 1958. It might have worked out conveniently for Moat, but there is factual evidence to suggest that he might have been struck by a derby curse. He scored three tries in three derbies for Hull against Rovers: he then played in four games for Rovers against Hull and was on the losing side in them all.

Peter 'Flash' Flanagan, a product of the city's Craven Street Youth Club, joined Rovers in 1960 and had a meteoric rise to prominence, gaining representative rugby league honours while he was still competing with Alan Lockwood for the hooker's berth at Craven Park. When the Robins transfer-listed him at £1,500 after 15 years' service, Flanagan dropped a definite hint as to what might be a convenient switch. "I would consider a move anywhere, but obviously the nearer the better," he said. He ended up joining Hull.

Ted McNamara, normally a full-back, signed for Rovers from Craven Street Youth Club in 1960 and made his debut in December 1963, but was released in June 1966. He moved to Wakefield Trinity with Rovers colleague John Bath, but had to work his passage back home, so he signed for Hull. And he said: "I enjoyed my spell with Kingston Rovers even though I was in the A team most of the time. But my time with Hull brought me the best two years of my life." It was not surprising, therefore, that his son Steve played for Hull on his way to attaining Great Britain international recognition although both have had links with leading National Conference League side Skirlaugh to the east of the city.

Prop forward Bob Coverdale joined Hull in June 1951 after playing locally for Boulevard Athletic and Electricity Works and went on to play in every game for Great Britain when they won the World Cup in France in the autumn of 1954. He was with the Airlie Birds as their 'great pack' developed, but the club transfer-listed him at £2,000 in January 1957. But it might have been very different because he had initially turned down Rovers and Halifax one season and then signed for Hull the next.

Coverdale, whose real forename is, oddly enough, Robin, moved to Wakefield Trinity, whom he captained, but at the end of December 1957 he moved back to his home city when Rovers finalised a deal to sign him in exchange for Sam Evans plus £2,000. And at the end of his playing career at Craven Park he became Rovers' A-team coach and assistant to coach Colin Hutton. And he recalled: 'I had a good time at Wakefield, but I wanted to get back to the Hull area and came back to Rovers. The players all knew that there would be a bit of needle in derby games and I often used to get called a few names from the terraces after I'd gone to Rovers. But there was always a good atmosphere for the derbies with the singing from the fans and all that went with them. And although there might occasionally be a few words exchanged between the rival fans behind the stands, by and large there was no crowd trouble at derbies.'

Sam Evans, in fact, came as close to anyone as achieving the East Riding treble in professional sport of playing rugby league for both Hull and Rovers and soccer for Hull City. He was actually born in Sunderland and soccer was his first love, but he just got as far as playing in the A team for the Tigers as an amateur. "I've always been a soccer man and my ambition was to play it professionally. I saw myself as a bit of a centre-forward, but then I was asked if I'd like to play rugby, so I had a couple of trial games with Rovers and in the end they asked me to sign for them. I found that rugby league was my sort of game. I was never all that brilliant, but I could catch and tackle, I could tramp and run a bit and I think I was also a good ball-handler", he said. Evans moved on to Wakefield Trinity and then joined the Airlie Birds, where he admitted: 'It was an honour to play in the same side such as Johnny Whiteley because he had such a brilliant rugby brain.'

Evans also served in the Household Cavalry for six years and worked as a doorman and a security officer, but he achieved further sporting fame as a wrestler and once fought 'Dr Death', better-known as Don Robinson, who had been on Rovers' books at one time and was later to become a successful chairman of Hull City. And there was a kind of compensatory sporting treble in East Yorkshire, which Johnny Whiteley, Cyril

Sykes, who was also a leading light in skiing at one time, and Peter 'Flash' Flanagan achieved. They were all involved with rugby league for both Hull and Rovers and played soccer for the Ex-Tigers, the organisation for former Hull City players. It was not quite the real thing, but it is as close as anyone has got apart from Evans.

In addition, Bill Riches played in Hull City's reserve team as a 17-year-old and had a spell of wartime soccer for Bournemouth, but played rugby while in the RAF. He was then invited to play for Hull against Batley in September 1944. Batley turned up a man short, so Riches turned out for them. Hull tried to sign him after the game, but he had signed for Batley at half-time and stayed with them for ten years! He captained Yorkshire and in 1953 there was a battle for his signature – between Hull and Rovers. He ended up at Hull this time, moving with Gerry Cox in a player-exchange deal before returning to Batley in December 1955.

At the same time there have been a few players who only just managed to play rugby league for both Hull and Rovers, a situation brought about by the introduction of substitutes. Ted McNamara, for example, played in one derby for Rovers in December 1963 and them made only one substitute appearance in a derby for Hull after moving to the Boulevard. Curiously, it happened on April 1, 1967, when he replaced Nick Trotter. And prop Phil Edmonds made one derby appearance as a substitute for John Millington in his Rovers days in March 1982 and then played in seven derbies for Hull between 1983 and 1986.

But one of the best examples of all concerns loose-forward Tracy Lazenby, who made two derby appearances for the Robins in 1983. He was replaced by substitute David Hall at half-time in the first and then substituted for Hall himself in the second. When he switched to Hull, he featured in one derby in April 1987 when he came on as a substitute for Lee Crooks after 60 minutes and was then replaced

Sunderland-born Sam Evans played for both Hull rugby league clubs and soccer for Hull City's 'A' team.

Ted McNamara signed for Rovers in 1960 but ended up at Hull via Wakefield Trinity.

Cyril Sykes, one of three men to have links with both Hull's rugby league clubs and soccer for the Ex-Tigers.

by Wayne Proctor 16 minutes later. He, therefore, played in a total of three derbies for the two clubs, but did not get a full game in any of them.

Others found themselves thrown in at the deep end if they moved to Hull or Rovers during the old summer close season because if often meant that they would make their debut for their new club in a derby match when the Eva Hardaker Memorial Trophy games took place during the pre-season build-up. Other players moved across the river and found themselves well and truly landed in it in terms of derby rivalry. Henry 'Ike' Mills, for example, played for Hull as a centre just before World War Two, but in 1946 he was transfer-listed at £250 at the age of 27 because he could not get a regular first-team game. He got his move on Christmas Eve, 1946, and joined Rovers, making his debut for them the next day against Hull! Mills, in fact, had played in his first derby for the Airlie Birds on Christmas Day in 1939. And he is in a select band of players who might be forgiven for having a warped sense of Christmas in terms of the spirit of peace and goodwill. George Bateman, Jack Hoult, Tom Danter and Bill Coulman also made their derby debuts for both Hull and Rovers on Christmas Day.

Perhaps, though, it was Len Casey, who made the ultimate sacrifice in the derby cause. Casey, usually a loose-forward, made his debut for Hull in September 1970, but crossed the river to Rovers five years later. He gained international recognition in two spells with the Robins, winning nine of his 14 caps with them between 1977 and 1983 and the other five while he was with Bradford

Len Casey (left) and Fred Ah Kuoi in their infamous derby punch-up in April 1984, watched by touch judge Keith Worrall.

Northern in between. He later coached Wakefield Trinity for 14 months until returning to Hull as coach in June 1986, staying at the Boulevard until March 1988. Casey was also an innocent victim of the ill-fated Scarborough Pirates venture before becoming a successful coach in National Conference League rugby with Beverley, the club for whom he had first played.

But Casey gained derby notoriety during his days with the Robins when he was sent off in the 46th minute of a league clash at Craven Park that ended in a 36-16 victory for his old club Hull in April 1984. Widnes referee Ron Campbell dismissed him following a fracas with Hull's hooker Neil Puckering, but that was not the end of the matter. Casey was immediately involved in a scuffle with the Airlie Birds' scrum-half Fred Ah Kuoi in which blows were exchanged and then he reacted to a comment made to him by touch judge Keith Worrall by pushing him as he left the field. As a result, Casey, who had been

Great Britain's captain, was given a six-month suspension that cost him a Premiership winner's medal and his international place on the summer tour to Australia. Casey took legal action to fight the sentence as one of the great derby soap operas unfolded. "It's history now, but if had happened in any other sport I'd have been a superstar because something was flashed on TV about it every week for a long time. It was the only fight that Fred's ever won and brought him to prominence, but I lost my international tour place and it ruined my career", he reflected.

Casey also pinpointed the possibility of a different outlook on derbies between local players and outsiders and tells a classic story to illustrate his point. He said: "In one of his early derbies Brian Lockwood looked round the Rovers dressing-room, saw what state some of the players were in just before the match and muttered: 'I don't know what's up with you codheads', which is what the West Riding lads used to call players from Hull. John Millington turned round and I thought he was going to throttle him. 'Millo' just told him: "It's all right for you, but it's a matter of life and death to us. We've got to live in this city and have to put up with everything if we lose – you don't!'…" Lockwood presumably got the message because he did win the Lance Todd Trophy in the all-Hull Rugby League Challenge Cup final at Wembley in 1980.

But it is a moot point in such a close-knit community and former Hull half-back Chris Davidson summed it all up succinctly when he said: "If you won a derby, it meant that you were kings of the city until the next one came round." Yet there certainly were all kinds of local pressures. Just before World War One, for example, it was reckoned that 11 Hull players and seven Rovers players all worked together at Earle's Shipyard in the city. Derby inquests should have been more than a little fascinating in that particular workplace the morning after the game before.

On reflection, it is probably surprising that Len Casey never became a Great Britain international while with both Hull and Rovers, but one of his contemporaries, Paul Rose, became the first player to do so. Rose, a former pupil of Hull's Jervis High School, set the record as the youngest professional to play for the Robins when he was aged 16 years nine months. He became a Great Britain international, had a successful spell in Australia with Dapto and then became unsettled at Craven Park. He was transfer-listed at £60,000, then £45,000 and finally moved for £30,000 in August 1982 – to Hull. And it turned out that he gained four caps with Rovers between 1974 and 1978 and one with Hull in 1982 to make his way into the local record-books.

Rose was always capable of looking after himself, but he does tell a story of a case of wrongful identity in a derby game. "Terry Clawson broke Alan McGlone's nose. It was the kind of thing that used to go on in open play at times. And when it happened, players just got on with it. But Alan was desperate for revenge in this instance. The trouble was that he thought I'd done it and spent all the game trying to get even with me," he said. Other stories, often hilarious in retrospect unless you were potentially the unfortunate innocent recipient, of mistaken identity have coloured derby history, while there have been numerous instances of coaches telling their players of their absolute necessity of subduing or even eliminating the opposition's derby danger men, but probably the names should remain anonymous to protect the guilty.

Rose also recalled a special means of preparation used at Craven Park. 'There would be a big bottle of sherry in the dressing-room and the forwards were expected to take a sip from it just before going out for a game because alcohol is supposed to be good for adrenalin. It was Harry Poole's idea when he was Rovers' coach and we used to do it for all the big games, especially the derbies', he explained. It is probably not surprising that Rose was later to become a popular publican in the Holderness village of Paull.

Paul Rose set the record as the youngest professional to play for the Robins. He also became the first man to be capped for Great Britain with Rovers and with Hull.

Colin Hutton was another outsider to serve both Hull and Rovers successfully in different capacities.

Len Casey receives his international cap from Rovers' chairman Bill Land in 1977.

There are plenty of other examples of the quirks of fate that have been thrown up for those players who have been prepared to risk the public ire by bridging the river to play for both Hull and Rovers. Life has had a habit of throwing up such instances at regular intervals in different circumstances. Really it has meant that everything has been pre-ordained for the fans in terms of unswerving loyalty, but nothing has been sacred for the players in terms of the right moves for their professional careers. As Ted McNamara admitted: 'I played in local derbies for both Hull and Rovers, but although I was brought up in East Hull, I was a Hull supporter and I've been a Black-and-White all the way through.' Billy Teall, who lives to the east in Bilton, summed up the rugby league religion in the city even more delightfully when he insisted at the age of 86: 'I was born in East Hull, but played most of my rugby on the Christian side of the river...'

All Square

I T IS commonly accepted in most sporting circumstances that local derby matches do not always produce the most classical, skilful play. The simple fact of life is that there is far too much at stake in such games for the two sets of participants. As a result, fear – of making mistakes and of losing – creeps insidiously in, negative thoughts are likely to abound and more often than not derbies tend to be games that offer little for the purists. They make up for that lack of quality, though, by the sheer passion, tension, drama and basic ebullience of the occasion. And for that reason alone they can never be classified as genuinely dull affairs even if a little quality might be missing.

It also means that they can frequently be close, low-scoring affairs because the players have a habit of developing a sixth sense that for once cuts out a lot of the risk factor. And if there is in general little difference in the overall ability of the two sides, it does mean that draws can be the order of the day.

It is a touch ironic in rugby league circles because the scoring systems that have prevailed over the years have dictated by their very nature that draws are a comparatively rare commodity. It is a philosophy that would go down well in America where there is a distinct school of sporting thought that basically just does not believe in them. They have even tinkered with laws and rules at times just to make sure that a draw cannot be the outcome. Those of us who have an in-built wariness of anything that emanates from our American cousins will gladly accept the necessary existence of draws and wonder what all their fuss might be about. After all, it naturally means that there has been more nerve-jangling excitement than usual for any game to end in a draw: quite simply, a draw has meant that the issue has been in doubt to the last, so does it really matter that there are occasions when honours ultimately remain even? Does it matter if, for once, there is no situation in which someone has to win and someone else has to lose?

The scoring systems in rugby league – regardless of the increase in points for a try and the decrease for drop goals – have also tested the simple arithmetic of any fan or participant because there is such scope for high-scoring games. But if a game lacks open rugby because of the fear factor and defences are on top of because of the prevailing negative ions, it does not in any way lessen the sense of occasion. And for the fans, a win is still a win over your closest rivals whether it be by the smallest margin possible or not.

And Hull's rugby league derbies have repeatedly mirrored the trend. They have produced their fair quota of low-scoring games with minimal victory margins and they have also produced a number of draws. These are occasions when the ritual after-match ribbing has to stop, but that is all. They will have still have kept everyone, including neutrals, on the edge of their seats. The first of them occurred in 1904 when a derby between Hull and Rovers ended 2-2 – not surprisingly, the lowest score for any draw between the two clubs.

The tone had been set with a series of close, low-scoring games since the first derby of 1899. That year Rovers won the second meeting 3-0; in 1901 they triumphed 3-2 and then lost 5-0 a little more than a month later; in 1902 the Robins again won 3-0, but the following year Hull won 3-2; and the first derby of 1904 had ended in a 7-2 defeat for the Airlie Birds. Instead of running up the proverbial cricket scores, they looked more like soccer scores.

But a draw finally ensued on December 10, 1904, in a game from which part of the proceeds were to go to the benefit of former Rovers centre Ernest Sleep, a Northumbrian who had been off work for more than a year after being hurt in a Durham county match. Curiously, he had never played in a derby game himself because he appeared just 11 times for the Robins and there was a certain amount of controversy surrounding the award of the funds, one argument being that the club should have made him a grant the previous season when they were better-placed to do so. In addition, Hull and District junior clubs postponed their matches so that their players could attend the game at Craven Street. But a heavy downpour caused the postponement of a boys' game organised as a curtain-raiser by the local schools' committee although the brass band did defy the elements. The weather also limited the attendance to about 4,000 by the start although it was later amended to 5,000.

The 15-a-side friendly at a time when Hull were known as the Blue and Whites included Rovers' latest acquisition, the 24-year-old Birkenhead and Cheshire county player Mullineux, but it was reported: 'The heavy going affected both sides and the exhibition was not one of the best. But then one never does expect anything classical from these local encounters. The play is too keen and the men lose their self-possession, not to mention their tempers. As a rule, the efforts of the players are more directed to the man than the ball and play suffers accordingly. When the ground and the ball are in the same condition as they were on Saturday, bad is made worse and it would be most unreasonable under such circumstances to expect to see the rugby game at anything like its best. A drawn battle was perhaps the most fitting conclusion because neither side could lay claim to an overwhelming superiority.'

As it was, there were no points in the first half and the second produced just two goals. Soon after the restart Mullineux had a 'try' disallowed before Jim Barry gave Rovers the lead with a drop goal after gaining possession following a scrum on Hull's line. His fondness for attempting drop goals often made him a controversial figure and it was observed: 'Barry's drop goal with such a soddened ball must be accounted somewhat lucky and it was not the game to attempt it even though it did come off. It spoilt his later work because he made similar attempts later on when he might have given the men behind a chance.' The circumstances surrounding Hull's equalising goal from Goodfellow hardly inspired the crowd, either, because it was reported: 'It was a perfect gift, Rovers being penalised right on their own line a few yards from the sticks at an easy angle. But Hull were decidedly lucky to be in such a position because the advantage had accrued from a rank bad attempt at goal by Goodfellow, whose shot had squirted so wide that it actually found touch near the corner-flag.' Another moan was that the fans had been given short measure with the first half lasting 28 minutes and the second 31. It all led to a certain amount of suspicion about the outcome because it was claimed: 'The man in the street expressed the opinion that the result had been pre-arranged, but the keenness of the play quite upset the idea.' The first derby draw had taken place, but it was, of course, unthinkable that there might have been any collusion or that both sides did not badly want to win on such an occasion.

There were further close encounters of the derby kind – Rovers winning 5-4 on Boxing Day, 1905, and Hull triumphing 8-6 in one of the early 13-a-side clashes on October 12, 1907 – before the next draw between the two clubs. It finished 8-8 on October 8, 1910, in what was the first league draw between Hull and Rovers.

This time the Robins were the in-form side, but there was extra interest created by the fact that Hull's winger Edward 'Ned' Rogers had scored in every derby held at the Boulevard to date against 'the wise men from the east'. Ground arrangements were stringent, too, because the open accommodation at the north-east corner of the enclosure, known as the Boys' Corner or the Chicken Run, was set aside for adults at an entry fee of one shilling. There was an extra bay in the best stand and a number of reserved seats, costing two shillings, on the cycle track. And a rope was put round the Boulevard enclosure at the Gordon Street end so that a lot of spectators could watch from near the dead-ball line.

The game attracted a 15,000 crowd and Hull initially led 3-0, but it was 3-3 by half-time. The second half was also drawn, leaving the final score 8-8. Rogers kept up his record with a goal to add to tries by Francis and Walton for Hull, while Rovers' points came from tries by former Salford winger Hyam and 'Dashing Dilly' Dilcock and a goal by Alf 'Bunker' Carmichael.

It was, in fact, amazing that there were only two derby meetings in 1910 and both ended in draws. The similarities did not just end there because the scores were level at half-time in the second meeting, too, and the referee for both games was Wigan's Ben Ennion, who had made a good impression when he had taken control of his first derby the previous year.

That second match was another league clash on Boxing Day and it ended 5-5 at Craven Street in front of a 16,000 crowd. In fact, there was a second-half stalemate in which no points were scored, but the so-called Cravenites had taken the initiative earlier on when William Dilcock, a youngster from Selby, raced over for a try, to which Carmichael added the goal. In this instance Rogers had to settle for setting up Hull's try for Boylen and Wallace made it 5-5 when he tacked on the goal.

William 'Dashing Dilly' Dilcock, a youngster from Selby, was prominent in the second match when both 1910 derbies ended in draws.

The early trend of tight, low-scoring derbies continued and some more close games followed – including a 7-5 win for Hull and games during World War One that brought the Robins a 6-3 success and the Airlie Birds a 6-5 triumph – before the next draw on September 27, 1919. The result might have been predictable on this occasion because the two sides went into the game with the same records of having won four matches and lost one so far that season, leaving them next to one another in the Northern Union table. It pitted one of Hull's all-time greats, Billy Batten, snr., against Rovers' Frank Bielby in the backs and attracted a crowd of 18,000, who paid record receipts of £1,065 at the Boulevard. And because there was a derby with plenty at stake locally as

usual, any thoughts of the national crisis created at the time by a railway strike took a back seat for a while.

It was the driving seat in which Hull soon found themselves during the game as they established a 6-0 lead with tries in a 10-minute spell by their two wingers, Francis and Nolan. But then the 'diehard methods of the gallant Reds' brought them back into contention against a Hull side who were becoming a powerful force in rugby. Tommy McGeiver, the former Leigh half-back, reduced the arrears with a try to make the score 6-3 and apparently render his inclusion as 'a subject for jubilation instead of being a matter for commiseration'. Hull centre Jim Kennedy landed a penalty to make it 8-3, but the Robins were level by half-time when Wootton touched down to leave Bradshaw with a simple conversion. Batten complained that 'the ball had never been in the scrummage' in the build-up to Wootton's try on a day on which the Airlie Birds also had two 'tries' disallowed. Rovers' bad luck came when a penalty by Bradshaw struck an upright, while Kennedy wasted several chances to win the match with a penalty. Apparently he was suffering from 'over-football' and 'eye and foot were out of harmony'. In any case there was no further scoring in the second half and it ended 8-8.

There was not to be another derby draw until Christmas Day, 1924, with the closest match in between being a memorable 2-0 win for Rovers in the Yorkshire Cup final in 1920. Hull were seeking revenge as part of the 1924 festivities because they had been soundly beaten 39-2 in early October by the Robins, who were the favourites to complete a double over their old rivals. This time, though, it was to be a much tighter derby at the Boulevard and the game failed to produce a try. Accordingly, it was reported: 'It was to be deplored that the scoring consisted of nothing more than penalty goals, but, truth to tell, neither side played as if they might register something more tangible.' But there was a crowd of 21,000 and most of them would not have minded how the points were obtained as long as their side either won or at least did not lose.

The Airlie Birds, who included new Scottish winger Cowan, conceded a number of early penalties and full-back Laurie Osborne gave Rovers a 12th-minute lead from one of them. But Hull's captain Jim Kennedy levelled the scores with a penalty of his own and then put his side 4-2 ahead with a second penalty eight minutes before half-time. Fifteen minutes after the break a scrum infringement enabled Osborne to kick his second penalty and that was how it stayed – 4-4. And the main bone of contention among the crowd did not concern the game itself because it was reported: 'During the first half there were many demonstrations and protests to the directors by the crowd in the well at the foot of the grandstand against their view being obscured by the spectators who had climbed over into the field of play. There was a lot of unnecessary encroachment and the referee refused to proceed with the game after the interval until the spectators were made to take up their old positions inside the railings behind the touchline.'

There were more tight, low-scoring derbies until the next draw on Boxing Day, 1927, at the Boulevard. Again there were no tries and no scoring at all in the second half and the score was the same as in the first derby draw in 1904 – 2-2. The weather was cold and windy and the attendance of 16,000 was thought to have been boosted by the cancellation of racing, while there was a notable absentee from Rovers' ranks – winger Lou Harris, who had played in all of the previous 18 derbies dating back to 1920.

The Robins had the wind at their backs in the first half, but immediately went behind after scrum-half John McIntyre had been penalised at the first scrum of the game and Hull full-back Ernie Jenney, who later became a director of the club, kicked the resultant penalty. Rovers hit back, though, and after 15 minutes Osborne equalised with a penalty given because of obstruction. Both sides were then disrupted with Jenney going off with severe concussion before half-time and Rovers having hooker Harold Binks sent off 15 minutes into the second half of a game that was described in derby tradition as 'more robust than scientific'.

Some of the derby trends were becoming remarkably familiar because there was soon to be another Christmas draw at the Boulevard and the score was again 2-2. There were no tries, of course, but the 10,000 crowd on Christmas Day, 1929, did at least see the two penalties spread over both halves!

There was some mitigation on this occasion, though, because it was reported: 'The state of the ground, on which stood pools of water in places, and the high wind did not contribute to fast and accurate football. Indeed, it was a wonder that the football was even so good under the fearful conditions and the players of both teams are to be congratulated for their heroic efforts.' Hull began with the wind at their backs and centre Joe Oliver gave them the lead after 15 minutes with a penalty awarded because of obstruction. Rovers then applied a lot of pressure and threequarters of the way through the match Oliver changed from hero to villain. He was caught offside and Osborne made it 2-2 with the resultant penalty.

Some of the derby draws had been tight enough and dour enough for no tries to have been scored and the sense of occasion had been an all-embracing factor. But on May 10, 1935, there was a derby draw with a difference – no goals were kicked instead! Another notable aspect of it was the poor attendance of just 2,100 at the Boulevard, probably because it was neither a league nor cup encounter. It was to decide the winners of the Hull Great War Trust Shield instead. And it suggested that there was a trend in terms of low gates because there had been only 3,500 to watch Rovers beat Hull 5-0 in a friendly in aid of the local unemployment fund in February, 1908, and crowds had dipped to the 2,000 mark during World War One.

This time the Airlie Birds led with a try by second-row forward Laurie Barlow after hesitation Rovers' defence, but 'Bunker' Wood dived over in the corner to make it 3-3. The Robins were then awarded an obstruction try after an infringement by Hull full-back Freddie Miller, but it was 6-6 when winger Billy Sheard touched down in the corner. Former Keighley winger Jim Sherburn

restored the Robins' lead when he also went over in the corner, but Hull's loose-forward Harold Ellerington set up a chance for Tommy Fletcher to score and make it 9-9 by half-time. The seesaw struggle continued with Tommy 'Tosh' McGowan scoring a simple try for Rovers, but Hull equalised in the final minute when Joe Oliver was again the hero as he scored in the corner and it ended 12-12.

Amazingly, there were no more derbies without a goal until the next draw. That came at the Boulevard on Christmas Day, 1950, when it was typically claimed that 'in the tradition of these derby games the game will not be remembered for good football'. Rovers held the upper hand, but failed to capitalise on the advantage of a second-minute try by Gerry Tait and Hull equalised when Roy Francis, who was to earn great renown as a coach with the club, went over in the corner after Johnny Whiteley and Ivor Watts had set up the chance. And that was the sum of the scoring as it ended 3-3.

Whiteley had just switched allegiance to become Rovers' coach when the two clubs drew again almost 20 years later in an Eva Hardaker Memorial Trophy clash at the Boulevard on August 14, 1970. It was a game that was to emulate one statistic from 1910 because it was the only other time that there were two derby draws in the same year.

The first draw of 1970 was on March 26 when Hull were searching for their third win of the season over Rovers. Phil Lowe returned to the Robins' side after a knee injury, while Ken Huxley came into the Airlie Birds' side at half-back because

Brian Hancock was ill for what was a Good Friday meeting in driving snow and strong winds at Craven Park!

Hull led after 15 minutes when Clive Sullivan scored in the corner, but Roger Millward made it 3-2 with a penalty after Alan McGlone had been penalised. Former Barrow forward Terry Kirchin, who had a point to prove to Lowe after being overlooked for the forthcoming tour to Australia, went over under the posts and John Maloney added the goal to give the Airlie Birds an 8-2 lead. The Robins then scored a controversial try when Phil Coupland appeared to knock the ball forward as he grounded it before Maloney kicked his 100th goal of the season to leave Hull 10-5 in front. But two minutes from time Rovers hit back to draw level. Millward, who had aggravated a groin injury, dived on the ball after Arthur Keegan had fumbled it near his own line and Terry Clawson kept his cool to land the conversion for a 10-10 draw.

Then came the second draw of 1970 and it was another of those games in which the scores were level at both half-time and full-time. But it was set against the backcloth of Whiteley's move to Craven Park, which was described as a bombshell by Hull chairman Charles Watson at the club's annual meeting three days before the game. Hull, who had just won the Hull Brewery Challenge Trophy against Swinton, brought in forward Chris Forster in place of Paul Ibbertson and welcomed back McGlone after an eye injury. They then had to make a late change because Dick Gemmell had a back injury, so Clive Sullivan made a rare appearance as a

Roger Millward, who played a leading role in the 1970 draw despite being injured.

Roy Francis, who featured in a derby draw in 1950.

John Maloney kicked his 100th goal of the season to put Hull in front in March 1970 but the result ended all-square.

centre. Rovers, on the other hand, were anxious to do well in their first game under Whiteley, who was fresh from a successful summer tour to Australia, but they were without new centre Ron Willett.

Millward gave Rovers an early lead with a penalty, but Sullivan sent in winger Howard Firth to put Hull 3-2 in front. Joe Brown added a drop goal to make it 5-2 before Lowe, who later went off with a shoulder injury, crossed for the Robins to make it 5-5 by half-time. In an absorbing second half Sullivan put Hull 8-5 ahead when he crossed under the posts and Chris Davidson added the goal. Millward kicked his second penalty, then sent in Ian Markham for the Robins' second try and added the conversion to put his side 12-10 ahead before Davidson equalised with a late penalty so that it finished 12-12.

The next draw on New Year's Day, 1975, was a clash in what was then rugby league's Second Division and provided a game of two very contrasting halves for the 7,052 crowd at the Boulevard. It was dramatic for one simple reason – Rovers led 10-0 at half-time and it ended 10-10 after Hull had mounted the most compelling comeback of any derby draw. Rovers' early advantage probably stemmed from the fact that they had just won the previous league encounter that season 19-12 at Craven Park on Boxing Day. Joe Brown had switched sides by this time and returned for the Robins, while Tony Geraghty was ruled out of the Airlie Birds' line-up.

Roger Millward, England's newly-appointed captain, gave the Robins a second-minute lead with a penalty after Len Casey had been penalised and then Clive Sullivan increased it with a 19th-minute try after Bernard Watson had sent him in. Hull were handicapped by an injury to Tony Banham and there was a major brawl before Rovers winger Ged Dunn raced 40 yards for an opportunist try on the stroke of half-time and Millward's touchline conversion made it 10-0 at the interval. It then became topsy-turvy as Hull centre Mick Crane took Brian Hancock's pass to score under the posts and Chris Davidson added the goal to make it 10-5. A further seven minutes later off-half Steve Lane nipped in for the Airlie Birds' second try and then 16 minutes from the end Davidson equalised with a penalty in front of the posts. Hull's transformation was such that on three occasions they almost snatched victory with drop-goal attempts, but it stayed at 10-10.

If that game was proof of the potential excitement of a derby draw, then the final one on October 7, 1979, exceeded most expectations because it was comfortably the highest-scoring of all. Hull had won five successive derbies, it was a clash between the previous season's First and Second Division champions, it took place at the Boulevard a little more than two months before the two sides were crucially going to meet in the final of the BBC2 Floodlit Trophy and it attracted a record First Division gate of 16,745. Steve Hartley and Brian Lockwood were back after lengthy absences for Rovers, who had just lost forward John Cunningham with a broken arm, while Steve 'Knocker' Norton played his first game of the season for Hull after suffering a groin injury while on tour to Australia and recent Welsh signing Graham Walters was on the substitutes' bench.

Another Welsh import, Paul Prendiville, opened the scoring for Hull after nine minutes and forward Charlie Birdsall added the touchline conversion. Clive Sullivan again haunted his old club when he went over after 16 minutes and Steve Hubbard took his turn to tack on a touchline goal to make it 5-5. Birdsall put the Airlie Birds back in front with a 24th-minute penalty and four minutes later Graham Bray scored their second try to make it 10-5. Then there was a three-minute period in which an almost carefree approach for once transcended a derby as the Robins scored tries through Allan Agar and Phil Hogan and Hubbard added the goals to put them 15-10 ahead at half-time. Three minutes into the second half Hubbard helped himself to a try and another conversion so that Rovers led 20-10. But back came Hull with substitute Keith Boxall going over and Prendiville adding the goal this time. And then they drew level six minutes from time as Walters enjoyed his derby debut when he, too, scored as a substitute before Birdsall made it 20-20 with the conversion. There was still time for a typical bit of derby drama when Huddersfield referee Billy Thompson disallowed a late drop-goal attempt by Hogan because it had touched Clive Pickerill's hand en route.

It was a game that confounded all the theories that derby matches were likely to be tight, low-scoring affairs, as a result of which there was a better chance of them ending with that rare rugby league element – a draw. That kind of result added even more tension and purpose to the basic derby theme because both sets of fans had been kept on tenterhooks in a more dramatic fashion than ever and the neutral spectators had gone home happier than usual. There again, it might all have been pre-planned on that occasion because that draw coincided with Hull A and Rovers A playing each other in a game that ended 12-12.

War Games

RUGBY league derbies in Hull have gradually taken on an all-encom- passing importance – even to the extent that everything seems to stop for them at the time in some circles and nothing will stop them, either. And even two World Wars could not totally expunge the derbies from the calendars. The clubs and their fans had to adjust and the war games – a strange term to apply to them at the best of times, of course, because of the significance that they took on – continued. Normally derbies brought two warring factors together in direct confrontation: it was perverse, therefore, that when most of the world were at war with each other that the derbies should take on the opposite hue and almost become as friendly as it was possible to be.

The fact that derbies continued during wartime probably did a lot for the communal spirit at a time of much greater strife and provided a necessary antidote to the horrors of war. In addition, their existence probably kept those who did not go to war in touch with routine and sanity. But it is notably perverse that the situation applied far more to one major war than it did to the other.

During World War One derbies regularly took place and created a tinge of normality amid the carnage elsewhere in the world. The powers-that-be probably took a shrewd note of that factor because there seemed to be more derbies than ever between Hull and Rovers at that time – five of them in 1916 and six of them in 1917, for example. The derbies kept going and in terms of morale probably did a fair bit towards keeping everyone else going, too.

But, strangely, if it were a humble source of comfort and solace to keep playing the derbies during the so-called Great War, then the situation did not recur the next time around. There were two derbies during successive days soon after the outbreak of World War Two, but that was it. There was a reason for calling a halt at that time and it was simply that Rovers decided to cease activities at the end of the 1939-40 season until peace returned. The end-product was that no derby between the Airlie Birds and the Robins took place between Boxing Day 1939 and Christmas Day 1945. This time war had actually eroded the tradition temporarily.

In 1939 there were just two derbies in two days after the outbreak of war and they took place against a certain amount of uncertainty about the continuation of rugby league in general during hostilities. In September of that year the new Lancashire-Yorkshire Emergency Rugby League took shape amid various stringent rulings. Matches were to be of 80 minutes' duration, but in no case less than 60 minutes. Gates were to be divided equally between competing clubs after the usual expenses and third-class return railway or bus fares for 15 players. And clubs were permitted to pay players ten shillings each per match to cover all meals and expenses except third-class rail or bus fares. Referees were to be allowed ten shillings expenses with five shillings for touch judges. Then there was the delightful dictum that that all clubs were expected to travel with full teams, but in the event of any team arriving short, it would be permissible to make up with any players available. And a club might play a player on another club's register if they were given permission to do so. Almost at once there was a revolt by players, led by those at Huddersfield, Halifax and Bradford, and they threatened to go on strike if the ten-shilling payment were not increased. The problem for the Rugby League Council was that they did not believe that the majority of clubs would be able to pay any more money.

It was against this backcloth that the two World War Two derbies went ahead with an 8,000 crowd watching the first of them at the Boulevard on Christmas Day. Rovers led after five minutes with a try by Alec Dockar and a conversion by George Carmichael, but Hull's winger Albert Bowers made it 5-3 with a 17th-minute try. The Airlie Birds went ahead with a try by second-row forward Jack Dawson, Freddie Miller tacked on the conversion and then Bowers scored his second try to make it 11-5. Moxon kept the Robins in touch with their second try, which Carmichael converted, and it was 11-10 to Hull at half-time. That was how it stayed.

Twenty-four hours later Hull completed a quickfire double when they won at Craven Park in front of a 6,000 gate although it was not until the closing

George 'Young Bunker' Carmichael was successful with his kicking in the first derby of World War Two at the Boulevard on Christmas Day 1939.

stages that they sealed victory. Rovers again scored first when they were awarded a try after three minutes as winger Jack Spamer was obstructed and full-back Billy Teall made it 5-0 with a penalty. Hull responded with two tries by centre Henry Mills, one of which Freddie Miller converted, and they led 8-5 at the interval. Teall reduced the arrears with his second penalty, but Hull scored two more tries in the final ten minutes for a 14-7 victory, Johnson seizing on a loose ball for the first and Mills completing his hat-trick – the sixth in derby history – when he dived over for the second.

But the first-ever war game had taken place at Craven Street on October 2,

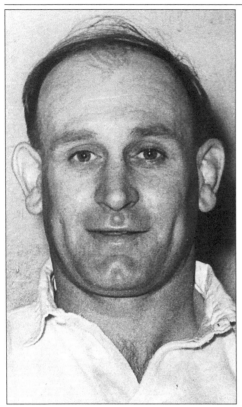

Henry 'Ike' Mills scored two tries in the second 1939 derby at Craven Park.

blame for Fussey's try, but, on the other hand, it was frequently mooted at that time that Rovers had made a big mistake in refusing him a trial when he had sought one so that their loss had been Hull's gain. On this occasion Rovers' only other points came from a try by centre Gilmore and a goal by Bradshaw.

The game at least attracted an attendance of 10,000 and the same figure was also given for the second derby in the War League in 1915. It set a trend because it was the first derby to be held on Christmas Day and the term 'soldier-players' had already become part of rugby league lore. Hull, who were defending an unbeaten home record, brought some of their squad into the city the night before the game, but Billy Anderson, who was travelling from Morecambe, did not play in the end. Hull reported 'brisk business in the booking of reserved seats at 1s 3d' and it was anticipated that every chair would be taken up on the day of the match, which lasted 70 minutes. And the East Hull Working Men's Committee of the Newland Orphans' Home collected £11 7s 8d for footballs for soldiers.

1915, as one of a continuous run of derbies throughout the conflict and it was reported that 'the quality of the game far exceeded the average in recent years'. Rovers' forwards battled hard and tackled strongly, but Hull's centres Billy Batten, snr., and Sid Deane, who had been earmarked as 'Darmody No. 2' after Steve Darmody, had too much invention and understanding in the end. All the points came from the backs and Rovers did score the opening try through winger Fussey, but they were 5-3 down by half-time and were eventually beaten 13-8. Hull ran in three tries from Jack Harrison and Alf Francis (two) and full-back Ned Rogers kicked two goals. There was a suggestion that Rogers had been to

The game was a one-sided affair after Rovers had lost centres Gilmore and Bradshaw with first-half head injuries and decided to utilise only four forwards. Hull lost Jimmy Devereux with a broken nose in the second half, but they had established an 18-0 lead by three-quarter time and went on to win 27-5 with Rovers' only points coming in the last minute when Fussey scrambled over for a try and Arthur Palframan landed the conversion. Hull, in contrast, scored seven tries thanks to Jim Kennedy (two),

Tom Herridge (two), 'Danny' Wyburn, Alf Francis and Billy Batten, snr., while Kennedy kicked two goals and Ned Rogers one.

There was another War League derby just 21 days later at Craven Street on January 15, 1916, and the 8,000 crowd saw another victory for Hull. Rovers had strengthened their side, but they were still lightweight in comparison with Hull, whose three tries all came from loaned players. To make matters worse, the first was scored by prop Frank 'Patsy' Boylen, who had been loaned to Hull from Rovers! Bruce and Stringer were Hull's other try-scorers, while Jim Kennedy kicked two goals. Rovers' only solace came from a goal by Billy Bradshaw in a 13-2 defeat. Once again there were casualties on both sides – Hull's Milner and Rovers' Huskins.

The hectic derby action of 1916 switched next to Good Friday, April 21, at the Boulevard and Hull again won. The 9,000 crowd were entertained by the Newland Orphanage Band and a further collection was taken for footballs as Easter gifts for the soldiers serving in France. But this time the war also meant that rugby league sides were including more and guest players: in fact, there were a few who played for Hull in the derby and then guested for Rovers against Salford on Easter Monday. Jim Kennedy recorded a try and a goal for Hull, whose other tries were from Alf Francis (two) and former York prop Tom Herridge. Rovers lost 14-8 although Gilmore scored two tries and Bradshaw landed a goal.

The surfeit of War League derbies and the loss of several recognised players

Jack Harrison scored a try in the first-ever war game at Craven Street on October 2, 1915.

from both camps began to take their toll in terms of attendances and there were only 6,000 fans at the Boulevard on September 23, 1916, to see Hull make it five wins out of five since the outbreak of hostilities. It was observed: 'The outcome of the abnormal conditions of the last two years has been to make the task of getting strong teams on the field a very difficult one and those who are conjured into existence cannot be regarded as anything like representative of the relative strengths of the rivals.'

But there was a curtain-raiser between Hull Melwood, the local Intermediate League champions, and a military team, which started 75 minutes before the main event, and it was the prelude to a scoring spree by Hull, who boasted seven different try-scorers. Rovers had struggled to assemble a side, but they took the lead with a try in the corner by Hulme after the start had been delayed for ten minutes to enable the crowd to settle. It was then Hull who began to settle, though, and they were 18-3 ahead by half-time. Alf Francis, Jim Kennedy, Billy Batten, snr., and Percy Oldham ran in tries, three of which Kennedy converted. Gregor Rogers, Jimmy Devereux and Billy Holder added further tries for Hull and Kennedy landed one more goal with Rovers' only response in a 29-6 defeat being a second try, which was scored by Arthur Moore. Batten and Tom Milner failed to complete the game for Hull, while Rovers were handicapped by the loss of full-back Holt, who had been injured in a scramble just before half-time.

Hull's sequence of eight successive derby wins was halted at Craven Street on October 28, 1916, by a Rovers side who went into the game without having conceded a try in their previous three games. The crowd numbered just 5,000 and they watched an Intermediate League game between Trinity and Southcoates beforehand as well as contributing to a collection for the interned Hull seamen's war charity. There was a further backcloth to the game in the form of a referees' dispute, which had originated in Lancashire and Cheshire, about the need to appoint neutral touch judges.

Rovers were weakened because of work commitments and there was little hint of victory for them in the early stages. Hull took the lead with a penalty by Jim Kennedy and, although Billy Bradshaw put Rovers ahead when he touched down after selling two dummies, the lead changed hands again. John Beasty scored a minute before half-time after Tom Milner and Tom Herridge had left him with an easy chance to give Hull a 5-3 lead. But it was all Rovers in the second half with Bradshaw landing a penalty after obstruction by Frank Boylen and then converting a try by Gilmore under the posts. Rovers then made sure of a 15-5 success with a further try by the remarkable 'Mucker' Clark, who had only one finger and a thumb on one hand because of a works accident during World War One. Bradshaw again supplied the conversion.

The dark days of war led to the abandonment of the next derby on Christmas Day, 1916 – when it began to get dark. It had lasted 63 minutes at Craven Street when 'darkness necessitated a curtailment of seven minutes' for the crowd of only 4,000. The decision was taken as soon as Hull scored to reduce the arrears, but they could have few complaints about it because they had delayed the start for 15 minutes to await the arrival of several players. As it was, both sides were below their normal strength because of other more pressing commitments.

It was only the third derby without a goal and the first without one in which both sides scored. Ned Rogers was one of Hull's late arrivals and Rovers took advantage of his initial absence to score their first try when Fred Oliver dropped on the ball as it rolled over the line. Their second try went to Billy Bradshaw, whose swerving runs had posed problems for Hull throughout, but he went off injured and soon afterwards Hunslet referee

Frank Renton called a halt. But Hull first made it 6-3 when Harold Garratt, whose brother Syd played soccer for Hull City, scrambled over for a try.

It was not until Easter 1917 – when snow was on the ground in Hull – that the next War League derbies took place. And those professional sportsmen who nowadays seem to want to be well-paid for playing fewer matches would doubtless have recoiled against the programme then faced by Hull and Rovers. They played each other on Good Friday and Easter Monday and also had games on the intervening Saturday. The two derbies attracted 5,000 crowds to the Boulevard and Craven Street respectively and produced two home wins.

Hull won 20-5 at the Boulevard with tries by Jimmy Devereux, Jack Holdsworth, Gregor Rogers and Frank Boylen and four goals from Jim Kennedy. They led 13-5 at the interval after Billy Bradshaw had scored a try and landed a goal for the Robins. The following day Hull beat Swinton 15-5 at home and Rovers lost 44-2 at Barrow before it was back to derby duty on the Monday.

Both sides made use of Swinton players as guests to complete their complements and the game started 20 minutes late. Hull led 5-0 after Holdsworth had sent in one of the guests, Talbot, and Gregor Rogers had added the conversion. Billy Bradshaw reduced the arrears with a penalty and then converted a try by Heathcote, who had followed up a kick, to give Rovers a 7-5 half-time lead. For the second derby in a matter of days the away side failed to score in the second half and this time Hull were depleted by the loss of one of their

guests, Evans, through injury. Newman made the most of it to go over unopposed for Rovers' second try and Bradshaw again added the conversion to give them a 12-5 victory.

It was indicative of the War League that 'Craven Street was selected by the secretaries' for the first derby of the following season on September 15, 1917. The attendance was only 4,000, but it was to be higher than those for the next four derbies and it was a 12-a-side match with only five forwards apiece, which was to be a feature for the rest of the war. Hull were without Billy Batten, snr., although they had insisted that he could not play for 'any other organisation', and Jimmy Devereux, who had been injured at work.

As it turned out, Rovers were weakened more than Hull by the start and soon afterwards they had a further setback when centre Boyd was injured. Hull went on to register five tries thanks to Mehew, the veteran George 'Rocky' Cottrell, Gomersall, Holder and Garratt, while Holder and Bill Kennedy kicked goals. Rovers replied with a try and a goal by Billy Bradshaw and a try by Empson in a 19-8 defeat.

The next derby was at the Boulevard on November 3, 1917, and took the place of a scheduled game between Rovers and York at Craven Street. Two days earlier the Yorkshire Northern Union's committee had held a special meeting in Leeds to hear Hull's objection to Billy Batten, snr., playing for Dewsbury because three months earlier they had withdrawn their permission, given in September 1916, for him to play for them. Dewsbury said that Hull could not revoke it while 'the present conditions of wartime football' existed. Hull won their case 'in view of the ambiguous terms of the permit', while Dewsbury escaped punishment although they had to pay their adversaries' expenses for the hearing.

Batten duly took his place in Hull's derby line-up for his first home appearance of the season in front of a crowd of only 2,000 and scored a try, but it was his fellow threequarter Jack Holdsworth who had a field day because he helped himself to five tries. Alf Francis also enjoyed himself with a hat-trick of tries as Hull ran riot to win 33-2 after the game had started 20 minutes late. By half-time it was 16-0 with two tries apiece for Holdsworth and Francis and two conversions by Jim Kennedy. Soon after half-time Holdsworth and then Francis completed their hat-tricks and Holdsworth added two more with Batten's try in between. Kennedy converted only Holdsworth's fifth try and Billy Bradshaw, who had been expected to be in Northampton instead of playing, landed a consolation penalty for the Robins in the last minute.

The attendance at the next War League game at Craven Street on December 8, 1917, was a mere 1,500 and the contrast was noted between 'the hundreds present and the corresponding number of thousands who might have watched the struggle under more peaceful conditions'. It was still a derby, though, and it was reported that there was still 'quite a liberal touch of old-time excitement'.

Rovers' young side battled pluckily and even led 10-8 at half-time. Jimmy Devereux gave Hull an early lead with a try, but Jimmy Cook equalised with an opportunist try for Rovers. A try by Billy Batten, snr., and a goal by Jim Kennedy gave Hull the lead again, but Newsome soon cut the deficit with a penalty and then half-back Kershaw dashed in for a try, which Smith converted. In the second half, though, Rovers were handicapped by injuries to Mulchinock and Frank Bielby and Hull went on the rampage after a try by Alf Francis had put them back in front. Batten, Bill Kennedy and Francis touched down for further tries and Jim Kennedy added one more goal as Hull won 22-10.

A certain amount of mystery surrounded the Christmas Day derby of 1917 at the Boulevard because it had originally been billed as a 15-a-side match played under rugby union rules between Hull and the Royal Naval Depot, who were to include several Rovers players. As it was, a traditional 12-a-side War League derby took place in front of a 2,000 crowd although Rovers included 'several of their soldier players'.

The game went ahead in a severe snowstorm and Hull made it four wins out of four that season. Rovers went ahead with a try by Frank Boylen, but Billy Batten, snr., touched down for Hull to make it 3-3. Hull led with a try by Alf Francis and a goal by Jim Kennedy before Frank Bielby scored another unconverted try for Rovers to leave them trailing 8-6 at half-time. The Robins again failed to score in the second half and Hull had the better of the poor weather conditions to win 14-6 with further tries by Newbould and Batten.

The next derby took place at Craven Street on February 9, 1918, and was

Hull FC at the outbreak of World War Two.

billed as the fourth meeting of the season between Hull and Rovers. In fact, it was the fifth – provided that the vagaries of the Christmas Day game allowed it to be counted as an authentic derby. There was an attendance of 2,000 and the match started 15 minutes late in cold, windy conditions.

Billy Bradshaw missed two penalties for Rovers before Jack Holdsworth gave Hull the lead with a well-worked try. But Rovers took advantage of having the wind at their backs and took the lead with a try by Kershaw, which Bradshaw converted. Two more Rovers tries followed before half-time – a solo effort by

Frank Bielby and one by Harrison – as they led 11-3, but yet again they failed to score in the second half. Martin, a guest loose-forward from Keighley, reduced the arrears to 11-6 before Hull's Bill Kennedy and Rovers' Frank Bielby were sent off in quick succession in what had become the first 11-a-side derby. Hull then produced a grandstand finale to win 20-11 with tries by Harris (two), Alf Francis and Jack Holdsworth, the last of which Newbould converted.

The final War League derby was a Good Friday clash at the Boulevard on March 29, 1918, and the complement of the two sides doubtless caused a few raised eyebrows among the 5,000 spectators who braved a strong wind to attend. For a start, Hull won again with the help of five players whom Rovers had dropped! Hull were particularly depleted as 'Government work claimed the majority of the absentees'. But both line-ups were liberally laced with guest players from the West Riding with Rovers including James Lyman, who had just earned county honours with Dewsbury. Players from both sides at least contributed a total of £12 at half-time towards the proposed Jack Harrison Memorial Cot for Hull Royal Infirmary.

Frank Bielby charged down a kick to give Rovers the lead with the opening try of a game which was apparently played 'on keen rather than scientific lines' and a penalty by Billy Bradshaw made it 5-0 at half-time. For the fourth successive War League derby Rovers did not score in the second half although they had to adapt to an injury to full-back Harrison. But Hull had taken a 6-5 lead by then with tries by Richardson and Giblin, ironically two of their guest players from Rovers, and that was how it stayed. Such generosity would end when the real war was over.

Christmas Crackers

FOR one reason or another, rugby league derbies in Hull have become increasingly rare in recent years. Divisional structures obviously make a difference, but tradition has, of course, insisted that they should be particularly big crowd-pullers at the main holiday times of the year. It often meant that Hull FC and Hull Kingston Rovers would take on each other at least twice a season – once at Christmas and once at Easter. As the years rolled by, Boxing Day and Good Friday became the customary dates in the diary for such meetings. But for a long time there was another big tradition – derby clashes on Christmas Day itself.

There also used to be a League soccer programme on Christmas Day at one time, but that concept died out – which is probably not surprising when you hear nowadays how footballers do little to offset their 'prima-donna' image by continually complaining that they play too many games and too many of them in close proximity to one another at Christmas and Easter. Curiously, they never seem to offer to take any kind of cut in their huge wages for playing fewer games.

But Christmas Day rugby league games lasted a little longer than they did in soccer circles and at one time derbies in Hull were accepted as annual occurrences even if they might always have understandably been deemed as being 'religiously incorrect' in some domains. And they meant, of course, that the tra-ditional Christmas spirit based on the ethos of 'goodwill to all men' had an even shorter time-span than usual. Christmases could be made or ruined depending on the outcome of derbies – and if your side had lost, all of a sudden it seemed to be a long time until you could seriously contemplate a prosperous new year. It was a case of a happy Christmas to everyone bar the opposition: there was no semblance of a goodwill truce.

Christmas Day rugby league derbies in Hull spanned a 53-year cycle and there is a classic sense of irony in the fact that the first such encounters should take place during wartime!

Hull won 27-5 in 1915, Rovers redressed the balance a year later when they triumphed 6-3 and Hull were victorious in 1917 when the score was 14-6. But the Christmas derby was to continue in peacetime and it became an accepted part of the rugby league calendar for a further 50 years with few exceptions for most of the time.

The 1918 Christmas Day derby took place amid General Election fever and was billed as a friendly at the Boulevard. Both sides still included guest players, as was the case 24 hours later when the two sides again met with Rovers appearing in green jerseys. It did not bring them the luck of the Irish, though, because they lost both games, going down even more heavily on Boxing Day when Hull won 29-2.

The Airlie Birds won the Christmas Day derby in front of 2,000 fans because of their superior finishing in an otherwise even game although players from both sides were short of match practice. Hull's five tries came from Billy Batten, snr., (two), Percy Oldham, John Beasty and Alf Francis, while Jim Kennedy landed three goals. Rovers' only reply was a try by Fussey and a goal by Bradshaw. Hull won 21-5 and the two derbies in two days brought the 12-a-side format to an end.

Normal league rugby had resumed by Christmas Day, 1919, and derby attendances had improved again with 14,000 fans visiting Craven Street on this occasion, some of them being forced to encroach on the pitch at one point. In fact, it was reported that the derby, which was part of a hectic festive schedule for both clubs, had been 'practically the sole topic of conversation on the docks and in the warehouses, workshops and offices of the city'. Hull made it 12 wins and one draw in the last 13 derby clashes in times of both war and peace and were at full strength, while Rovers' absentees included their injured skipper Wootton.

Rovers again failed to take their chances and Hull went ahead when Jim Kennedy crossed under the posts and Ned Rogers tacked on the conversion. Winger Alf Francis then went over in the corner and Jack Holdsworth's try made it 11-0 to Hull at the break. Rovers hit back with a try by Arthur Moore and a conversion by Billy Bradshaw, but Kennedy scored his second try and then landed a penalty to give Hull a comfortable 16-5 success.

Rovers returned to winning ways in derby games by winning the Yorkshire Cup and the following month they visited Hull on Christmas Day, 1920. The game attracted a record derby crowd of 25,000, which was hardly surprising in view of the fact that Hull were the reigning play-off champions, Rovers were at the top of the league and memories of the dramatic Yorkshire Cup final had scarcely faded. Above all, it was reported that most of the fans 'had actually passed through the turnstiles!'

Although there was to be one major derby to take place in 1920-21 after the two clubs had finished next to each other at the top of the league, it was suggested that Rovers' Christmas triumph meant that they were 'fully entitled to the mythical derby Ashes for the season'. In fact, the festive frolic was a personal triumph for their diminutive centre Gilbert Austin, who was to appear in 24 successive derbies at one point. He opened the scoring with a try after intercepting a pass by Ned Rogers and Sandy Gibson added the conversion to make it 5-0 at half-time. Jim Kennedy cut the deficit with a penalty for Hull, but Austin produced a vintage solo effort for his second try towards the end. Kennedy landed a second penalty, but Rovers survived Hull's late rally to win 8-4.

Hull and Rovers were both title contenders when they next met on Christmas Day. It was at the Boulevard in 1922 in front of a 20,000 crowd and Hull officials had to protect the pitch with straw so that it was playable after heavy rain during the build-up to the game.

The Airlie Birds made a positive start to go 8-0 in front after just 12 minutes as

Edgar Morgan scored the first try, which Jim Kennedy converted, and then winger Billy Stone sprinted over in the corner. After half an hour Rovers hit back when John McIntyre went over in the corner from the base of a scrum and it remained 8-3 at half-time. Jack Hoult reduced the deficit further with a try for the Robins, but Hull made light of having to face the wind in the second half and Morgan went over in the corner for his second try. They increased their lead when scrum-half Eddie Caswell robbed McIntyre to score under the posts, Kennedy landing the conversion, and then went over in the corner in the closing stages as Hull completed a 19-6 victory.

There was another 20,000 attendance for a Christmas Day derby in 1923 and the crowd included soccer players from Newcastle amateur side Walker Park, who had played Hull City's reserves earlier in the day and were the guests of Rovers' directors at Craven Park. Rovers were without the injured Jimmy Cook and Frank Bielby, but winger Louis Harris passed a late fitness test, while Hull recalled Harold Bowman and Bob Taylor to their pack.

The Christmas philosophy of goodwill disappeared on this occasion as Rovers were soon reduced to 11 men. Billy Westerdale was dismissed for 'charging' Ned Rogers and leaving him with a damaged nose and then another forward, Frank Boagey, was sent off after an incident which resulted in Hull's hooker Brennan having to be carried off. Rovers were already 5-0 in front thanks to a try by loose-forward Harold Binks and a conversion by Laurie Osborne and that was how it stayed in the first half.

Eddie Caswell, who increased Hull's lead in a 1922 derby at the Boulevard.

The second half developed into an absorbing contest as the Robins, who also lost 'Mucker' Clark temporarily because of injury, defied the odds and made the most of having the wind at their backs, initially going further in front with a try by Arthur Moore after he had kicked ahead. Hull's Welsh left-winger Emlyn Gwynne followed up his own kick to make it 8-3, but then Jack Hoult scored Rovers' third try and Osborne added the conversion. Gwynne then became only the third player to score a hat-trick of tries in derby rugby as the Airlie Birds recovered to 13-9, but Gilbert Austin went over in the corner and a goal by Osborne sealed an unlikely 18-9 victory for the Robins.

The Christmas Day derby of 1924 ended in a 4-4 draw at the Boulevard, where a 20,500 crowd saw Hull end a run of six derbies without a win the following year. An hour before the start there was a curtain-raiser between unbeaten Hull FC Juniors and Kingston Juniors, which was organised by Hull Old Boys' League.

Rovers took the lead with an 11th-minute penalty by Laurie Osborne after Hull had been caught offside, but half-back Stanley Whitty responded when he kicked ahead and dribbled over the line

Rovers' Billy Westerdale gets in his kick despite the attentions of Hull's 'Tommy' Bateson end Edgar Morgan in a 1925 derby. Two years earlier Westerdale had been sent off in a Christmas derby game.

to score to leave it 3-2 after a first half punctuated by penalties. Three minutes into the second half Bob Taylor took his turn to dribble over for the first of his two tries for the Airlie Birds, but after 57 minutes Osborne made it 6-4 with a penalty after John Beasty had been penalised for obstruction. Taylor snapped up his second try just after the hour mark and that was how it stayed as Hull held out for a 9-4 success.

It was exactly a year later that the next derby took place with 20,000 packing into the Boulevard in 1926. It was later disclosed that those who actually paid numbered 19,486. Hull, who were without full-back Ernie Jenney because of suspension, were seeking a 39th successive home win, but it was to be a low-scoring game and took the aggregate of points in the last four derbies to just 36. This time the curtain-raiser was between Boulevard Juniors and New Albion in the 16-18 League.

Hull's home record only just survived because they were behind after 18 minutes when Laurie Osborne landed a penalty following an offside infringement. But six minutes later Harold Bowman beat his own teammate Bob Taylor in a race to the line to touch down before the ball went out of play and that was the end of the scoring. Defences dominated and Hull had to settle for a 3-2 victory despite going close to two more tries in the second half.

The next Christmas Day derby in 1928 was another low-scoring affair. Hull were without their influential forward Bob Taylor and Rovers' star was in the ascendancy because they were challenging for the league title. The 14,000 crowd included the Rugby League secretary John Wilson, a former Scottish international cyclist who had joined Rovers' board in 1906, five years after moving to East Yorkshire. Born in Kelso, he joined the Rugby League Council in 1918, he was the Great Britain business manager on their tour of Australia and New Zealand two years later, playing in an emergency, and he was the Rugby League secretary until his retirement in 1946.

Rovers went ahead after 20 minutes when Harry 'Scrubber' Dale exchanged passes with Jack Spamer before touching down. Ten minutes later Spamer helped himself to a try and the Robins remained 6-0 for the rest of the first half. Loose-forward Arnold 'Tommy' Bateson made it 6-2 with a penalty for Hull soon after the resumption, but an injury to Whitty caused them to reshuffle their formation and there was no further scoring.

The 1929 Christmas Day derby at the Boulevard ended 2-2 and there was yet another low-scoring game the following year. It attracted a 16,000 crowd to the Boulevard and they saw a tough, physical game even by derby standards with Christmas spirit and festive bonhomie at a premium because it was reported: 'From a football point of view, the match cannot be said to have been highly interesting: nor can it be said that it was exceptionally clean. Far too much friction and recklessness was shown by both sides and the natural conclusion was that casualties were numerous. In fact, there was hardly a player who did not get a few hard knocks in the course of a very strenuous needle match.'

Hull opened the scoring after 20 minutes when full-back Ernie Jenney gathered a kick by John McIntyre and dropped a goal, the ball bouncing over after hitting the bar. Five minutes later Hull's winger George Bateman went over in the corner for an unconverted try and it was still 5-0 at half-time. With Rovers' stand-odd half Jonty Parkin having an off-day with his kicking, Hull increased their soon after the resumption with the best move of the match as Bateman scored his second try when Joe Phillipson carved out the opening. It finished 8-0 and the main casualties were Rovers' Hill with a fractured collarbone and Parkin with a broken bone in his hand, while Bateman suffered severe concussion after a collision with Saddington.

The Boulevard tradition continued in front of an attendance of 14,000 a year later in 1931, but this time it was Hull who failed to score. Both teams had been inconsistent and the big hope was that it would be 'a good game free from unsavoury incidents'. Hull had Harold Bowman back in their pack after injury and called up Billy Metcalf and Fred Winsor, but full-back Ernie Jenney was an injury absentee. Rovers had Jonty Parkin back as Harry Dale's half-back partner, but Jack Spamer was missing because of a bruised thigh and Billy Westerdale came into the side.

Rovers' Billy Batten, jnr., was hurt early on, but he recovered in time to see his side go ahead when Dale set up a try for his partner Parkin. There were the customary casualties with Hull's Metcalf and Joe Oliver and Rovers' George Saddington and Harold Binks also taking knocks. But the Robins were 7-0 in front at half-time after full-back George

Carmichael had landed a penalty and then dropped a goal. In the second half Rovers' prop Les Sharpe followed up his own kick to score his side's second try and they ran out 8-0 winners.

It was 1934 before there was another Christmas Day derby and it turned out to be a high-scoring match by recent standards for the 15,000 fans the Boulevard. Hull preferred Harold Ellerington at loose-forward to Jim Courtney, while Rovers were depleted in the backs and that proved to be their downfall.

The Robins soon led with a penalty by Harry 'Chazzer' Beaumont, but Hull went in front with a try by Ernie Herbert and a

Freddie Miller, who starred in some memorable Christmas derbies either side of World War Two.

goal by Freddie Miller. Ted Tattersfield landed a second penalty for Rovers, but the Airlie Birds scored two more tries thanks to Joe Oliver and Herbert and Miller added the conversions to give them a 15-4 advantage. Harry Dale slipped through a gap for Rovers' first try and Harry Beaumont tacked on the goal, but Hull took command after the interval with tries by Cecil 'Dicky' Fifield, Oliver and Ellerington. Oliver converted Ellerington's effort before Rovers grabbed a second try when Billy Batten, jnr., went in at the corner, but it was not enough to save them from a 26-12 pasting.

There was another 15,000 crowd for the Christmas Day derby of 1935, but for once it took place at Craven Park. Precautions were taken to guard against frost with four tons of salt being applied to the pitch, followed by a thick layer of straw. Ernie Herbert passed a late fitness check for Hull, while Rovers, who had gone five derbies without a win, were again without the suspended Joe Evans. They tried a new half-back partnership of Welsh import Whitton and Harry Beaumont, while John 'Mick' Eastwood returned after a lengthy absence.

Hull were on their way to becoming the league title and championship play-off winners, but they were made to fight all the way by a Rovers side who were hindered by an injury to Whitton early in the second half. The Robins again led initially with a penalty when Wilf McWatt made the most of an offside infringement after seven minutes, but Joe Oliver equalised with a penalty given for obstruction. But the Airlie Birds led 8-2 at half-time after two tries by Welsh winger Clarrie Gouldstone, whose career

was ruined by shoulder trouble, and nine minutes into the second half Oliver kicked another penalty. But the Robins hit back with a try by winger 'Bunker' Wood and it was not until 11 minutes from the end that Oliver secured a 15-5 victory when he ran threequarters of the length of the field to touch down for a try that Freddie Miller converted.

It was back to the Boulevard for another low-scoring Christmas Day derby in front of 20,000 fans in 1936. Hull's new winger Davies was injured, so Eric Overton deputised, while Rovers gave derby debuts in the backs to Welsh import Perrott and Norman Foster.

The game was fought at a fast pace and Hull simply led 6-0 by half-time with three well-struck penalties by Joe Oliver. Early in the second half winger John Eastwood crossed in the corner for the only try of the match, but Wilf McWatt's conversion attempt struck the woodwork and Rovers were unable to redress the balance further as Hull won 6-3. Eastwood, Ray Maskill and Jack Spamer all took knocks to add to the Robins' woes.

Hull had not been beaten in ten successive derbies when they met Rovers in front of a 17,000 gate at a foggy Craven Park on Christmas Day, 1937. The Airlie Birds had lost the services of Cecil Fifield, but welcomed back Harold Ellerington after injury. There were derby debuts for Hull's Australian winger Frank Hurley and Rovers' winger Harrison and former Goole forward Jim McNulty.

Hull led after 22 minutes when centre Sid Wilson scored under the posts and Joe Oliver added the conversion. Oliver then followed up his own kick to touch down and landed a penalty before Hurley crossed in the corner, but Rovers cut the gap to 13-2 with a penalty by Wilf McWatt before the interval. Hurley and his fellow winger Bob Corner ran in further tries for the Airlie Birds, but the Robins hit back to make it 19-5 when Fred Shillito touched down in the corner for their only try of the day. But then Hurley completed his hat-trick and Oliver converted an interception try by Jack Dawson to give Hull an emphatic 27-5 triumph.

Hull won the next Christmas Day derby 11-10 at the Boulevard in the War League in 1939 and hosted the first post-war derby exactly six years later in front of 15,000 fans. And it was agreed that the gate receipts from the game, which

Ivor Watts, who scored the Airlie Birds' first try in a War League derby.

ended in semi-darkness, would be pooled between the two clubs. Hull were without Alec Dockar because he had travelling difficulties, but another forward, Charlie Booth, snr., passed a late fitness test. Rovers were without half-back Emlyn Richards, their recent signing from Welsh rugby union club Mountain Ash, because he was stationed in Norfolk with the RAF, but they gave a chance to Viv Hill in the forwards.

The game was a personal triumph for Hull's winger Tommy Glynn, who became the first player to score four tries in a derby, as they trounced Rovers, who were weakened by injuries to Wilf McWatt and Arthur Bedford, 25-9. The Airlie Birds, inspired by Albert Bowers, led 11-3 at half-time after Ivor Watts had registered their first try and Glynn had scored his first two. Bernard Spamer converted Watts' effort, while Sid Atkinson touched down for Rovers. Winger Horace Gee kept the Robins in touch with their second try before Glynn completed his hat-trick and Spamer added the conversion. Atkinson crossed again for Rovers, but Jack Tindall, Watts and Glynn completed the scoring with three unconverted tries.

Hull hosted their first-ever all-ticket match at the Boulevard in front of 14,000 fans on Christmas Day, 1946. Rovers had let a half-time lead slip in the Yorkshire Cup semi-final against Hull a little more than two months earlier and this time there was an uncomfortable action replay for them.

Rovers' Wilf McWatt and Hull's Freddie Miller exchanged penalties in the opening 20 minutes. Miller added a further penalty before Emlyn Richards put the Robins 5-4 ahead at the break with the first try of the match. Sid Hattersley charged over to nudge the Airlie Birds back in front with their first try and Miller landed a third penalty as they won 9-5.

The Christmas Day derby of 1947 was at Craven Park and produced another 9-5 home win in front of a 15,000 gate. There was a curtain-raiser between East Hull Intermediates and Barnsley United. Hull brought Arthur Bedford into their pack, while Rovers were without full-back Wilf McWatt, who was injured.

Rovers won against the odds and their jubilation was underlined by the fact that Richards, their two-try hero, was chaired from the field at the end. There was no scoring in the first half, but the Robins took command with Richards' tries and one by Bill Jackson. Hull had to settle for a last-minute try by scrum-half Bob Jewitt, Freddie Miller adding the conversion.

Rovers were seeking their fourth successive derby win when they went to the Boulevard on Christmas Day, 1948, for a game that attracted another 15,000 crowd, but it was not to be. Hull welcomed back scrum-half Duncan Jackson, while Rovers were without Maurice Daddy, who had a shoulder injury.

Rovers ended up with a much bigger casualty list because they finished with only 11 men after Henry 'Ike' Mills and Harold Welsby had been injured, while Cyril Smith, Joe Ramsden and Wilf McWatt also suffered knocks. Hull's full-back Tom Hart kicked two first-half penalties and their Australian winger Bruce Ryan touched down on the stroke of

Next page: **Tommy Finn, who made his derby debut on Christmas Day, 1954 and turned out to be one of Hull's most notable scrum-halves ever.**

half-time to make it 7-0. After the interval Bernard Madden and Hagan Evans ran in further tries for Hull, Hart landing one conversion as it finished 15-0.

The Christmas Day derby of 1950 ended in a 3-3 draw at the Boulevard, but Hull won at Craven Park in front of

13,500 fans exactly a year later. The Airlie Birds were the clear favourites because there was a big gap in the league between the clubs and Rovers had not won at home since September 15. Hull's loose-forward Johnny Whiteley passed a fitness check on an injured arm, while Rovers included half-back John McAvoy, their recent signing from Warrington, and Arthur Palframan, jnr., in preference to Frank Moore and Jim Barraclough, who had had a lengthy absence with a broken arm.

Rovers had won all six post-war derbies at Craven Park at that point and they made Hull fight all the way for their success because it was poised at 8-8 at the interval. The Robins lost George Forth because of injury, but led 6-3 with three penalties by Ronnie Mills after Ivor Watts had opened Hull's account when he scored in the corner. Roy Francis scored the Airlie Birds' second try, which Tom Hart converted, before Ron Armitage dropped a goal for the Robins before the break. Hart converted a try by Australian winger Keith Gittoes before Mills made it 13-10 with his fourth penalty. But Don Burnell made it 4-0 in Hull's favour in terms of tries and Hart kicked his third goal as it finished 18-10.

There were 11,000 at the Boulevard on Christmas Day, 1952, when Rovers, then struggling near the foot of the league, turned the tables on Hull on a muddy pitch in perfect weather. The Airlie Birds' winger Ivor Watts was serving a one-match suspension, while the Robins were without Henry Mills because of an eye injury, so Dennis Rushton lined up against his old club.

Hull scored all their points in the first half with a 34th-minute try by Roy Francis and three goals by Tom Hart and led 9-4 at the break after Alec Dockar had landed two penalties for Rovers. John McAvoy scored the Robins' first try after 49 minutes and 20 minutes later Dockar's penalty made it 9-9. Dockar's fourth penalty nudged Rovers in front two minutes from time and then there was a dramatic finish. Francis was close to his second try, but McAvoy gained possession instead and raced away to touch down for the second time himself, Dockar's conversion making the final score 16-9.

But a year later Hull emphatically completed a hat-trick of derby wins in 1953 when 12,500 fans saw Rovers go down to their heaviest defeat in the series since November 1917. Hull welcomed back second-row forward Harry Markham, who had been sidelined since being hurt on international duty for England against France at Odsal in early November, and player-coach Roy Francis, but Rovers' influential half-back Bryn Knowelden was unfit.

Hull opened the scoring with a penalty by Colin Hutton and a try by Ivor Watts, who was to become only the second player in derby history to score four in a game. Bernard Conway and Watts crossed for two more tries in a three-minute period midway through the first half and Hutton converted them both to make it 15-0. Scrum-half Albert Tripp scored the Airlie Birds' fourth try after 31 minutes before Brian Beck landed a penalty for the Robins three minutes before the interval. Rovers did not fare much better with the wind at their backs in the second half and Mick

Scott touched down for Hull's fifth try after 57 minutes to make it 21-2. Six minutes later Hutton converted Bob Coverdale's try and then Watts completed his hat-trick, making it four six minutes from time when he crossed in the corner. In 1917 Rovers had lost 33-2: this time it was 32-2.

The next derby was on Christmas Day, 1954, when Hull again won, but there was a crowd of only 8,500 to see it. And they saw a derby debut for Hull by a trialist from Lancashire, who turned out to be one of their most notable scrum-halves ever, Tommy Finn. Rovers, meanwhile, gave a derby debut to full-back Pat O'Leary against his old club, but were without the injured Bernard Golder and Keith Goulding, influenza victim George Ellenor and the unavailable Geoff Tullock.

Johnny Whiteley put Hull in the driving seat when he set up two tries – for Tommy Harris after four minutes and Harry Markham in the 26th minute. Colin Hutton kicked one conversion, but Rovers hit back with winger Dennis Rushton crossing in the corner and it remained 8-3 in the first half. Centre Brian Beck burst through for the Robins' second try and Hull had to hang on grimly until Whiteley and Finn scored two tries in the last eight minutes. Hutton contributed another goal as Hull won 16-6.

Rovers must have had a sense of *déjà vu* when they went to the Boulevard for the 1956 Christmas Day derby. It was a throwback to three years earlier as 12,500 fans saw them lose heavily to a Hull side inspired by Ivor Watts. The Airlie Birds, then second in the league,

decided not to risk Keith Bowman after injury, while former Welsh international forward Tom Danter played for Rovers against his old club for the first time because Ken Pickersgill was unavailable. Peter Key and Sam Evans returned for the Robins, who were without Tom Bourton because of an ankle injury.

It was amazing that Rovers led after five minutes when Terry Buckle landed a penalty because of an offside infringement and it was amazing that they were only 3-2 down at the break after Tommy Finn had dived over for Hull in the 30th minute. The Airlie Birds changed their shirts at half-time because of the muddy conditions and it seemed to pay dividends because they went on the rampage with Watts, who had set up Finn's try, again scoring four tries in a Christmas Day derby, the first three coming in a 10-minute spell early in the second half. Rovers' winger Brian Shaw was hampered by a knock, but there was no stopping Hull and Rowley Moat darted over for their fifth try with Colin Hutton landing his first conversion to make 17-2. The Robins then had Key carried off with a facial injury, Hutton landed a penalty and Watts crossed for his fourth try. Hull then took their tally of tries to eight thanks to Carl Turner and Moat and Hutton tacked on a conversion as they finished 30-2 ahead.

A crowd of 16,000 saw Hull win the next Christmas Day derby at the Boulevard in 1958. Both clubs' preparations were hampered by dense fog that prevented their out-of-town players from attending training, while Rowley Moat, who had scored for Hull in the last Christmas Day derby, was in the Rovers

Muddy action from the Christmas Day derby in 1963.

Christmas Day. The 12,000 crowd were treated to a curtain-raiser between youngsters from East Hull and West Hull to raise funds for Hull Schools' Rugby League. But it was not a happy return home for the Robins because the Airlie Birds won their ninth successive derby on a muddy, boggy pitch.

Hull had eight players cautioned, but Rovers failed to take full advantage of their many penalties and paid the price for it. Peter Bateson put the Airlie Birds 4-0 ahead in the first with two penalties and the Robins were unable to get back into the game. Eddie Wanklyn, whose son Wayne played League soccer for Reading and Aldershot, increased Hull's lead with the first try after 51 minutes when he crossed in the corner and then Jack Kershaw sold a dummy for the sec-

Paul Longstaff, who cost £7,500 and was the centre of attention at a 1967 Christmas Derby.

side at centre after a spell in-between at Oldham. The Airlie Birds welcomed back centre Brian Saville, who had been sidelined with a broken collarbone, while Ray Gill was called up on the wing. The Robins' leading try-scorer Brian Coulson took his place on the wing after recovering from illness.

Ivor Watts recorded another Christmas Day hat-trick for Hull, three times putting a foot in touch as he looked destined to score! It meant that there was only one try throughout when Tommy Harris sent in Johnny Whiteley for the Airlie Birds in the second half and Peter Bateson, who was preferred to Arthur Keegan, added the conversion to put the final touch to their 11-2 victory. Bateson had been responsible for giving Hull a 6-2 half-time lead with three penalties although Rovers had again been the first side to score when Cyril Kellett landed an 11th-minute penalty.

Rovers were back at Craven Park for their home derbies in 1959 after a spell of hosting them at Boothferry Park by the time that they next clashed with Hull on

Hull's David Doyle-Davidson halts Rovers winger Mike Blackmore on Christmas Day, 1965.

ond to make it 10-0. Cyril Kellett reduced the arrears with a penalty for Rovers, but Hull ran out 13-2 winners after Brian Saville had touched down to complete the scoring.

There was then a break in the Christmas Day derby tradition and Rovers made the most of it when it resumed in 1965 in front of a crowd 8,500 at the Boulevard. Hull included four teenagers – John Maloney, Gary Pearson, Shaun O'Brien and Mick Harrison – and preferred Kevin McGowan to Ken Foulkes, who had been out of action with a shoulder injury, at scrum-half. Rovers gave a derby debut to new signing Brian Wrigglesworth in the centre and tried a new half-back partnership of David Elliott and Mike Stephenson, but they were without hooker John Shaw because of suspension.

In November 1920 Rovers had beaten Hull 2-0 in the Yorkshire Cup final in the lowest-scoring derby ever: this time the two sides equalled that statistic. Bill Holliday landed the winning penalty for the Robins after eight minutes, but their nerves might have been calmed because he and Arthur Mullins missed seven other such opportunities between them on a sticky pitch.

Rovers had the edge over Hull when the two sides met on Christmas Day, 1967, in front of 11,800 fans at the Boulevard. They had already beaten them three times in different competitions that season and the festive derby provided them with their fifth successive win in the series. The main interest surrounded their new centre Paul Longstaff, who had cost a club record £7,500 from Huddersfield, because he made his debut in a derby after the postponement of a game against St Helen's earlier in the week. But Hull were without centre Dick Gemmell, whom they had just re-signed from Leeds for a £4,000 fee.

Ironically, it was Bill Holliday, Rovers' previous record signing at £7,000, who did the damage with his kicking. Peter 'Flash' Flanagan scored the Robins' only try after seven minutes, but Holliday kicked six goals, three of them in each half, and Hull became increasingly frustrated. Five minutes from time they had scrum-half Chris Davidson sent off and their only replies were a second-half try by winger Norman 'Nobby' Oliver and three goals by John Maloney, Gemmell's replacement. He kicked one first-half penalty and added two more goals after the break, but Rovers ran out 15-9 winners.

A cheekbone injury forced Dick Gemmell to miss out on a Christmas Day derby again in 1968, while Norman Oliver was in Hull's side after rejecting a move to Featherstone Rovers and Howard Firth returned on the other wing. But the 10,000 crowd at Craven Park were probably more intrigued by Rovers' line-up because they included Australian World Cup forward Arthur Beetson in the second row. Beetson, an ironworker in a Sydney shipyard, had been signed on a short-term deal from

Arthur 'Artie' Beetson recovers from his Christmas injury in hospital.

Rovers' prop Steve Wiley is challenged by Hull's Chris Davidson in December 1969.

Balmain a little more than two months earlier. At the same time the Robins had also snapped up Sydney policeman Jim Hall, a prop forward from Penrith, and he was on the substitutes' bench for the derby. In addition, Colin Cooper, who had just recovered from a groin injury, was given the scrum-half berth because Roger Millward had a damaged shoulder and Alan Burwell had a broken hand, while Cliff Wallis was a late replacement for Terry Major at loose-forward.

Rovers' Phil Lowe (left) gets the ball away during the Boxing Day derby in 1970 despite being harrassed by Hull's John Maloney.

Hull's Clive Sullivan beats Rovers' Cliff Wallis to score in the Boxing Day derby in 1970.

Quite simply, Wallis had better luck than Beetson. After Terry Clawson had put Rovers ahead with an 11th-minute penalty, Wallis scored the only try of the game from a pass supplied by Beetson, whose derby career was to last just half an hour, however. He was carried off with a broken leg after one of his powerful runs had been halted and Hall replaced him. The Robins went on to win 9-0 after Clawson had kicked a second penalty four minutes from the end and Hull also had their casualties because Chris Forster

damaged a thumb and Mike Harrison suffered a shoulder injury. But Beetson's plight was ironic because he had been sent off against Huddersfield at Craven Park at the start of the month and it was expected that he would be suspended for the Christmas derby. But his hearing was cancelled, leaving him available for the

Hull prop Shaun O'Brien dives over the line for a try on Boxing Day, 1970.

Phil Coupland scores Rovers' only try in a derby in December 1971.

derby in which fate ended his brief Rovers career. Early in 1969 Beetson and Hall returned to Australia although they were back in East Yorkshire as recently as last year for a testimonial function for the Robins' Mike Fletcher.

That derby, though, was the last of the many to be played on Christmas Day.

They continued to be a regular part of the holiday programmes at Christmas, New Year and Easter, but it was probably felt that Christmas Day should be spent in a little more subdued and sedate mood. Big Artie Beetson would probably have echoed that sentiment.

Rovers' Derek Windmill makes a break in a Boxing Day derby in 1972.

Far, far away

DURING the long, dark winter nights there is no longer a professional rugby league season to provide sustenance. The 1990s saw a revolution in the code that included a dramatic switch to summer play, so it would not be entirely surprising nowadays if a fan's fancy turned to something else during the winter. One substitute pastime might be to turn the attention towards sports quizzes, either as a potential questionmaster or for a wager with a friend or even in a more-organised league. And if needed, one intriguing question might always stand out for those devotees interested in the history of rugby league derbies in Hull: Which game between Hull FC and Hull Kingston Rovers took place the furthest distance away from the city?

There were local games on neutral soil at nearby Boothferry Park, there were trips to West Yorkshire to watch derbies at Headingley and there was the memorable day in May 1980 when the two sides took each other on in the final of the Rugby League Challenge Cup amid the twin towers at Wembley. But real local rugby aficionados will know the answer to the poser – Penzance. In fact, two other derbies between Hull and Rovers took place much further afield than Wembley and much nearer Penzance – at Camborne and Falmouth. Does it mean, therefore, that there is a part of that foreign field of Cornwall which is forever orientated to rugby

league? In the summer of 1962 there certainly was a glorious attempt to attempt to spread the gospel of rugby league in one of England's more remote counties.

The Airlie Birds and the Robins became missionaries of the code during that close season by playing three so-called friendlies in Cornwall. The fact that the most remote game of the three matches took place in Penzance is particularly significant for the simple reason that the town is the birthplace of Graham Paul.

At that time Rovers had signed a number of rugby union players from the West Country and Paul turned out to be one of the greatest of them. He joined the Robins from Penzance and Newlyn rugby union club as a half-back in November 1958, but made his name as a speedy winger and soon earned himself the nickname of 'the Cornish Express'. A corporal in the RAF, with whom he also had a reputation as a middle-distance runner and long-jumper, Paul was reported to have switched codes for £1,500 after Rovers officials had watched him play a representative game for Cornwall against Gloucestershire in Bristol.

And it was no coincidence that Paul, who still lives in Newlyn after retiring as a publican, made most of the arrangements for the summer trip to Cornwall in 1962. In fact, it worked out well for the tour, if not for Paul himself when he was sidelined towards the end of the 1961-62 season.

Graham Paul, nicknamed the 'Cornish Express', in full flight.

He explained: 'I was injured just before Easter against Wigan when I broke my collarbone on David Bolton's head! Because Rovers were so keen for the tour to go ahead, they asked me if I'd go back to Cornwall to organise it, so I took it over while I recovered from my injury. There were three main things to sort out – getting the pitches, finding hotels that would take the two parties and getting the goalposts.

'Getting the pitches and the opposition wasn't too bad, but it was difficult to find hotels because of the reputation of some of the rugby union clubs at the time. And they weren't going to be too willing to take two rugby league clubs who had a tradition of being at each other's throats most of the time, but eventually I got them billeted out to the

Graham Paul dives over for a try for Rovers. He was one of a number of players signed from the West Country and turned out to be one of the greatest of them all.

Land's End Hotel, which is now a steak-house.

'There was also a bit of a problem because all the pitches in the area were owned by the local councils and then leased out to the rugby union clubs. In the summer the grounds went back to the councils, but the posts went back to the clubs because they belonged to them. So I went to a local builder's yard where I had a friend called Wilfred Edwards, who made some posts for us and made sure that they were erected at the ground, which was a huge help. When the tour was completed, I went to see him to find out how much he was owed, but he didn't charge us a thing. He said it had been a great pleasure to have everyone from Hull down in Cornwall and besides he had just sold the goalposts to Penzance and Newlyn – my old rugby union club!'

So the stage was set for a trip into the rugby unknown. Hull and Rovers both took 17-strong squads of players plus officials for what was described as 'a three match-missionary tour in a hotbed of rugby union football'. Rovers officials had spent some months organising it all, but the most curious aspect of the whole escapade was that there would have been no derby matches at all if their original plan had come to fruition. The Airlie Birds as a whole were substitutes – for Halifax! Hull had been asked to step into the breach only when Halifax, the organisers' first choice to go with the Robins, pulled out.

The two parties set off on June 2, 1962, staying overnight in Bristol before completing the journey to their headquarters at Land's End. And the venture had attracted a certain amount of interest in the West Country because of televised rugby league matches and the departure of other prominent players from rugby union into the professional code. And Mike Blackmore, the former Devon county threequarter and England rugby union trialist who had just completed his first season at Craven Park, stopped off in Plymouth to record a television interview about the tour. But two of the Robins' other converts from rugby union, Ted Bonner and Jim Jenkin, also a former Penzance and Newlyn player, ironically missed the trip because they could not get away from their teaching duties.

It was also necessary for the two parties to take plenty of rugby league supplies with them as they left nothing to chance. They transported 10,000 souvenir programmes, detailing the personalities and history of both teams, corner-flags, admission tickets, buckets and sponges and even a cobbler's last with spare studs for boots. Furthermore, Hull and Rovers officials agreed to act as gatemen with a player from each side acting as the touch judges for each game, while there was, of course, one other neutral observer – Warrington referee Charlie Appleton, who took charge of all three matches.

Between them they all produced three remarkably high-scoring derbies by any standards and the switch to summer rugby league that was, of course, a precursor of the trend that was to become the order of the day in the mid-1990s. In fact, the tour meant that derbies between Hull and Rovers had taken place during every calendar month of the year. June

Terry Hollindrake and Terry Devonshire each scored three tries in the exhibition derby at Penzance in June 1962.

completed the set because at that point one isolated derby had taken place in July when the Airlie Birds beat Rovers 13-5 in a Peace Day celebration in 1919.

The first meeting in Cornwall took place on June 4, 1962, in Penzance on a bone-hard pitch in front of a crowd of 2,300. Even though the usual physical tone of a derby clash was noticeably missing as both sides did their best to produce an exhibition of open rugby played at pace, there were plenty of minor injuries caused by the condition of the pitch and both sides finished the game with 12 men because of them. It was, of course, not the usual reason why either side might finish short-handed in a derby clash!

The game produced a total of 19 tries with Hull, who ended up with eight different players on the scoresheet, winning 57-26. The Airlie Birds' try-scorers were Terry Hollindrake (three), Terry Devonshire (three), Dick Gemmell (two), George Matthews (two), Mike Smith, Tommy Finn and Bill Drake, whose brother Jim captained Rovers, while Arthur Keegan (six), Hollindrake (two) and Matthews kicked goals. The Robins' tries came from Brian Tyson (two), Arthur Bunting, Graham Paul, Brian Hatch and Brian Burwell, while Cyril Kellett landed four goals.

The next day the rugby league derby roadshow moved on to the spacious ground at Camborne and Hull again won on another bone-hard pitch in front of 1,500 spectators. There was a strong, cold wind balanced by the evening sunshine for a little more competitive game as Rovers tried to equalise on the tour. They were not far from achieving their object, either, because they were only four points in arrears with five minutes remaining, but Hull ran in two late tries to earn a 38-26 victory. The Airlie Birds' tries came from Keith Barnwell (three), one of which stemmed from a spectacular run from inside his own half, Terry Devonshire (two), Terry Hollindrake (two) and David Doyle-Davidson, while Arthur Keegan landed seven goals. The Robins ran in six tries from Brian Hatch (two), Albert Thompson, Peter Murphy, Brian Tyson and Arthur Bunting, while Cyril Kellett contributed four goals.

The concluding tour game was at Falmouth, where amazingly the 2,000 crowd was augmented by the crews of two sea-going tug-boats from Hull who had just docked in the town! They enlivened the atmosphere, indulging in some good-natured heckling of referee Charlie Appleton to remind him of what derbies were really like, and saw Hull make it three wins out of three on tour with a 44-31 triumph. For the second successive game all four members of the Airlie Birds' threequarter line scored with Terry Devonshire contributing three tries, Dick Gemmell two tries and a goal, Terry Hollindrake one try and five goals and Keith Barnwell two tries. Their scoring was completed by a try from Bill Drake and a try and a goal from Cyril Sykes. The Robins' points came from tries by Albert Thompson (two), Harry Poole (two), Brian Hatch, Arthur Mullins and Graham Paul and five goals by Cyril Kellett.

Stories, which may be true, exaggerated or just plain apocryphal, abound about the tour. For example, Hull's Arthur Keegan was supposed to have been barracked in Cornwall by a supporter of Peter Bateson, his great rival for the club's full-back berth, and one rugby union addict is said to have complained vociferously about the lack of punch-ups from their friends from the North! And Graham Paul was paid an unheard-of derby compliment for his role in organising the tour because he recalled: "George Matthews, who was playing stand-off for Hull, told me that he if I stepped inside him, he would let me go over for a try under the posts so that I could say that I'd scored in rugby league in my home county!" Was this really the stuff that derbies were supposed to be made of?

But Paul, in fact, has a generally harmonious recollection of the tour because he added: "To be perfectly honest, the relationship between the two teams was terrific. They travelled together on the same coach with the directors and other officials on another one. I didn't go into the clubhouse at Penzance after the game there because I didn't want to cause any waves after changing rugby codes, so I went down to the Navy Inn nearby to chat to one or two people. So much for my diplomacy! I soon found out that the rugby union players had taken the rugby league players into their clubhouse and then the rugby league players had invited the rugby union players back to their hotel at Land's End. All in all, it was a great experience."

Paul, who was a publican at the Rugby Hotel and the Avenue Hotel in Hull and then the Sportsman at Heamoor, near Penzance, before retiring, now contents himself with games of golf and bowls although he does still help out with the

Rovers' centre Terry Major touches down in September 1962.

Hull's Brian Clixby brings down Rovers' Harry Poole in September 1962.

Hull full-back Arthur Keegan, watched by teammate Tommy Finn, just manages to tackle Rovers' Graham Paul into touch in March 1964.

junior and mini-rugby sections at his old club Penzance and Newlyn after finally having his amateur rugby status restored after 33 years! And he and everyone else can muse about the fact that, from a marketing standpoint, the three-match rugby league tour to Cornwall in the summer of '62 may not have made substantial inroads, but they certainly provided the respective factions in Hull with some derbies with a difference.

A chase for possession in a derby in October 1964.

Rovers' Len Clark touches down in a derby in March 1964.

Charity Fare

THE fundamental concept of a local derby match in any sport is that the rivalry between the two teams and their supporters is so intense that it should always be at fever-pitch. They are based on the traditional belief that no quarter should be asked or given, no prisoners are taken and it is very much a question of the survival of the toughest, both mentally and physically. If the demands of the occasion were anything less, then they would lose everything in terms of character, tension and drama.

The 1962 tour by Hull and Rovers to Cornwall might have suggested otherwise because of its general conviviality, but it is surely a contradiction in terms to contemplate the possibility of there being anything remotely charitable about derby meetings in the normal course of events. But a lot of the rugby league clashes between Hull and Rovers have, in fact, had charity as an integral quality to go with the fans' unyielding faith and hope of the occasions. The reason for such a strange dichotomy is that rugby league has traditionally been played in tough, industrial areas where a sense of spirit, common bonds and a community feel have always abounded, particularly in all kinds of troubled times. There has been a close-knit atmosphere in which generosity of spirit and wallet have been interwoven amid the austere landscapes that have supplied the backcloth to the code. It is not simply a case of having to play hard and work hard: it has also been possible to give hard. It is a prevailing social condition that dictates that nothing is too much trouble for your friends. And even if it might have gone slightly out of fashion during the grasping, material 1980s, it has thankfully not altered too much at all in rugby league circles.

As the years have passed, there has been a charitable background to many of the derbies between Hull and Rovers. For example, in 1906 there was fund-raising for the local unemployed, in 1929 there was a joint benefit match and in 1950 there was a friendly for the Jack Townend Memorial Trophy, named after the Hull FC hero who, in 1900, had been the first player in derby history to score a hat-trick of tries in a game. But there was a classic example of charity beginning at home in one series of derby clashes because they took place to help with the development of the code locally and it led to the annual game for the Eva Hardaker Memorial Trophy.

The Hardaker name made a major impact in sport both nationally and locally. Alan Hardaker, a modest soccer player from Hull, went on to become the secretary of the Football League for many years and he was at helm for a number of far-reaching changes. His brother Ernest, meanwhile, was the strong, demanding driving force behind Hull FC at the same time as being chairman of the club. After playing occasion-

Ernest Hardaker, the driving force behind Hull FC.

The Eva Hardaker Memorial Trophy was always a pre-season game, taking place in either July or August, and it did not attract the biggest crowds because it took place at the height of the holiday season and its very essence suggested that it was likely to be a less-competitive derby than usual. But it kept the derby tradition alive: in 1976, for example, it was the only clash between Hull and Rovers during the calendar year. It also gave fans of both sides a handy excuse when discussing the outcome. If your side lost, then it was just a routine pre-season warm-up game that bore no meaningful resemblance to anything that might happen in the more competitive winter months: but if your side won, it was still a derby success over the old enemy, it started the season off on a bright note and it put the opposition on the defensive in terms of local status. In fact, the games threw up a remarkable amount of interesting features and quirky situations. They did, for example, often carry the extra burden for close-season signings made by both Hull and Rovers that they were likely to be thrown in at the deep end to make their club debuts in a derby atmosphere.

The inaugural Eva Hardaker Memorial Trophy match on August 6, 1960, produced plenty of points and pointers and attracted an 8,000 crowd to the Boulevard. Rovers' international forward John Taylor had the chance to return to action following a broken leg in the Yorkshire Cup after building himself up thanks to his work as an PT instructor in the Army based at Catterick, while his colleague David Elliott had broadened his horizons by playing rugby union at his forces unit in

ally for Hull A, he had become a shareholder in 1924 and then joined the board 20 years later. He was at the helm during the emergence of Hull's 'great pack' of the 1950s and one of those forwards, Jim Drake, recalled: 'We were lucky that we had a very, very strict chairman in Ernest Hardaker. He was very Victorian in his attitude and he was a very good, straight and honest man. He also had the ability to make you feel that you were one of the lads. We were all raw teenagers when we joined the club, but he taught us how to behave ourselves and helped us to change from boys into men.'

But two days before Christmas in 1959 Ernest Hardaker's wife Eva died and her name, ironically, was to remain to the fore in local rugby league longer than that of her better-known husband. That was because a one-off annual local derby was added to Hull's sporting calendar so that funds might be raised for local rugby league.

Hampshire. Both obtained leave to play, winger Bob Harris and prop Eric Thundercliffe made their senior debuts and in the centre Rovers had Joe Drake, whose more-illustrious twin brothers Jim and Bill were in Hull's line-up against him for the only time in a derby. Hull gave a chance to promising youngster Colin Mountain at full-back and Ralph Walters, who played for both clubs, got the hooker's role in preference to Tommy Harris.

Hull had won ten derbies on the trot, but Rovers were to be the first winners of the trophy as they soon established their authority and led 21-6 soon after half-time. Full-back Cyril Kellett showed no rustiness as he kicked seven goals, while Terry Major, Bob Harris, Ray Jaques and substitute Arthur Bunting crossed for the Robins' tries. Hull made the final score more respectable at 26-16 as Cyril Sykes landed two goals and threequarters of their threequarters – Gordon Harrison, Terry Devonshire and Stan Cowan – scored tries, as did second-row forward Mike Smith, who had earned fame by making his debut for the club in the 1959 Rugby League Challenge Cup final against Wakefield Trinity.

The next Eva Hardaker Memorial Trophy game took place at Craven Park on August 12, 1961, in front of 9,000 spectators and included two interesting derby debutants – former Devon county rugby union forward Ted Bonner for Rovers and Malcolm Storey, who had been signed from York junior rugby, for Hull. In addition, the Airlie Birds included Peter Bateson, who had decided to come out of retirement, and Tommy Harris and Brian Saville, who has spent the summer recovering from injuries.

Mike Smith, a try-scorer for Rovers in 1977.

The annual game had by now been dubbed a 'prestige' affair, but this time it was a full-blooded clash with plenty of cautions and hard knocks. Hull enjoyed most of the possession and led 5-0 after 13 minutes thanks to a try by Frank Broadhurst and a conversion by Bateson, but that was to be the end of their scoring. Cyril Kellett again came to the fore, landing two penalties, helping to set up tries for Arthur Bunting and Bob Harris and converting them both so that Rovers emerged as 14-5 winners.

Hull won the trophy for the first time on August 11, 1962, as they followed up their hat-trick of triumphs in the exhibition matches in Cornwall two months earlier. The tour apart, Rovers had won the previous four derbies, but this time they came to grief in front of a 9,500 crowd at the Boulevard. There was an experimental look about both packs with the spotlight on Cyril Sykes in Hull's second row because he had been out of action for eight months with cartilage trouble.

It looked ominous for Hull when Cyril Kellett put Rovers ahead with a penalty after five minutes and he kicked two more of them by half-time. But by then the Airlie Birds had edged 10-6 ahead with tries by Wilf Rosenberg and Charlie Booth, jnr., and two goals by Arthur Keegan. Hull then took control to

Arthur Keegan scored two goals when Hull won the trophy for the first time in 1962.

go 25-6 in front with three tries in five minutes – one from Sykes and two from Terry Hollindrake – and Keegan converted them all to end up with more goals to his name than Kellett for once. Rosenberg added his second try, while Rovers' only try came from Bob Harris and Kellett kicked his fourth goal. Hull, though, paid a heavy price for victory in what might have been viewed in some quarters as a mere pre-season warm-up game because skipper Johnny Whiteley was hurt midway through the second half and it was later revealed that he would be absent for six weeks with an Achilles tendon injury.

Rovers were the favourites to regain the trophy on August 17, 1963, because they had a strong pack at their disposal. Most significantly, Harry Poole was back in the second row after being out for nearly a year with a broken leg that he sustained in the Yorkshire Cup final, but Cyril Kellett, Jim Drake and Terry Major were injured and Alan Burwell was unavailable, so Brian Burwell was called up. Hull did not risk injury victims Peter Whiteley, Cyril Sykes and Terry Hollindrake and Jack Kershaw was ill, so they brought in Charlie Nimb and gave a chance to 20-year-old loose-forward Frank Johnson, whom they had signed from York junior rugby.

Rovers soon took command in front of a 9,000 crowd at Craven Park and went into a 16th-minute lead when Mike Blackmore touched down. Len Clark missed the kick, but made amends with a penalty before Graham Paul scored following a flowing movement to make it 8-0. Terry Devonshire reduced the arrears with a try, which Arthur Keegan converted, before the interval, but soon after the resumption Paul touched down again to make it 11-5 in a game that was notable for the generally-high quality of its tries. The point was proved as Hull mounted a famous fightback to score two more well-taken tries. Devonshire touched down for his second, Malcolm Storey dashed 50 yards to score and Keegan tacked on two more goals to leave the Airlie Birds as 15-11 winners. The injury jinx struck again, though, because Rovers' winger Bob Harris damaged a knee and Hull prop Jim Macklin dislocated his shoulder. But it was a derby match, so he had it put back immediately and continued playing!

Rovers gained their revenge in ruthless style a year later when they won 35-14 at the Boulevard on August 15, 1964, in the first derby since the introduction of two substitutes for injured players and some new scrummaging laws. The Robins gave Chris Young the chance to stake a claim for the winger's role vacated by Graham Paul following his retirement and they preferred Alan Holdstock to Peter Flanagan at hooker, while Eric Palmer was ill and David Elliott had an injured thumb. Hull brought in close-season signing Ken Huxley at stand-off half, while the Sullivan brothers, Clive and Brian, played in the same derby line-up for the first time.

But the game was dominated by the presence of the Robins' big former rugby union prop John Bath, who scored two

Hull hooker Alan McGlone is halted by Rovers' Harry Poole (left) and John Bath in the 1964 Eva Hardaker Memorial Trophy meeting.

Rovers winger Bob Harris goes in for one of his tries in the 1964 game.

third Rovers player to score two tries, while Alan Burwell contributed one. Hull had their moments with tries by Kevin McGowan and Brian Sullivan, while Arthur Keegan landed four goals. This time Clive Sullivan suffered an injury to his shoulder ten minutes from the end, allowing Terry Devonshire to come on as the first derby substitute.

Rovers were the favourites for the next Eva Hardaker Memorial Trophy clash and they wanted to do make an early impression at Craven Park because five of their first six games were at home. It took place on August 16, 1965 – on a Monday evening instead of the more traditional Saturday afternoon – and it attracted a record gate of 12,000 for the series of matches. The Robins welcomed back winger Graham Paul after his retirement had lasted a year, while both sides gave opportunities to promising forwards: Hull included teenager Mike

early tries, both of which Cyril Kellett converted. Rovers had 20 points on the board by half-time and Kellett had 20 points of his own by the end with two tries and seven goals. Bob Harris was the

A casualty station for Hull during the 1965 Eva Hardaker Memorial Trophy game.

Rovers' David Elliott streaks away for the only try of the 1965 game.

Harrison because Jim Neale was injured and Rovers chose 19-year-old Keith Pollard because Brian Tyson was missing with knee trouble.

A scrappy game produced only one try, scored by Rovers' half-back David Elliott in the 17th minute. It was enough to give them the edge as they had most of the possession and went on to win 11-6, but the rest of the scoring was handed over to the goalkickers. Cyril Kellett and Bill Holliday landed two each for the Robins and Eric Broom kicked three penalties for the Airlie Birds. Paul was the major casualty on this occasion because he tore his hamstring, while Hull's Terry Devonshire, Kenny Foulkes and Broom all received knocks.

By the 1966 meeting in the series, which was at the Boulevard on August 12 in front of a 5,428 crowd, Hull were seeking to set the record straight because they had lost three successive derbies in

Cyril Kellett was successful with six goal attempts out of seven in the 1966 Eva Hardaker game.

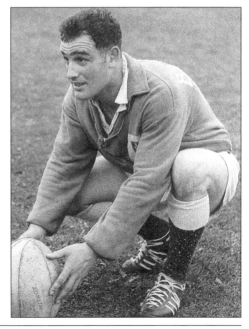

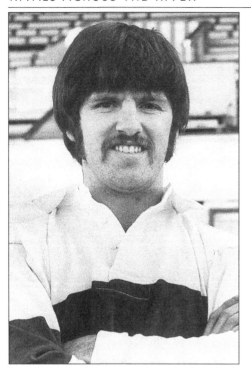

The 1966 game was a personal triumph for Mike Stephenson, then 19, who ran in a hat-trick of tries.

1965, including a 31-5 defeat that had given Rovers their biggest win over them since 1924. Hull were without Arthur Keegan, who was still on tour in New Zealand, and Terry Devonshire, but they welcomed back forwards Jim Neale and Frank Johnson, who had been injured in the latter part of the previous season. Rovers also had an absent tourist, Peter Flanagan, so his place at hooker was taken by Joby Shaw.

But there was no revenge for the Airlie Birds because they were heavily beaten again in a game which was a personal triumph for the Robins' 19-year-old utility back, Mike Stephenson, who was to move across the city to join them in the latter part of his career. Stephenson ran in a hat-trick of tries and Cyril Kellett was successful with six goal attempts out

of seven as they accounted for 21 points between them. Substitute Arthur Bunting and Chris Young also crossed for tries for Rovers, while Hull's only reply was a second-half penalty by John Maloney as they lost 27-2 after being 12-0 down at the interval. One of their few influential players on the night, Alan McGlone, was the injury victim on this occasion and Brian Clixby replaced him.

There was a new twist to the proceedings on August 15, 1967, because it was a case of third time lucky after the traditional summer pre-season game had to be postponed when the Craven Park was twice waterlogged after torrential rain! Accordingly, the game had to be switched to the Boulevard, where 5,610 fans watched it. Rovers, seeking their fourth consecutive victory in the competition, included Australian winger Alan Smith in place of Greg Ballantyne, while Charlie Booth, jnr., was on Hull's substitutes' bench because there had been doubts about his availability.

The change of venue did not benefit Hull because they were again beaten and it was a nightmare occasion for their normally-reliable goalkicker John Maloney, who failed with all seven attempts. The Airlie Birds had to be content with what was regarded as the try of the match from Terry Devonshire to add to two touchdowns by Joe Brown, but the Robins were able to rely on Bill Holliday for four goals, while their centre Alan Burwell stole the show with a hat-trick of tries. Chris Young chipped in with the first try of the night for Rovers as they won 20-9.

The next Eva Hardaker Memorial Trophy meeting took place on August 5,

Howard Firth in possession in the 1968 game as Rovers' John Moore covers.

1968, in front of a gate of 5,895 at the Boulevard with Hull's Clive Sullivan, fresh from a successful stint with Great Britain's World Cup side, opposing his tour colleague, Rovers' Chris Young. There was more interest in the Airlie Birds' other winger, though, because they had just signed him from local rugby union side Hull and East Riding for a reported £3,000 fee. After the game he was unmasked as Howard Firth, a 22-year-old PE teacher from the Doncaster area, who had been a prolific scorer after joining Riding from Thornensians. As an athlete, he had recorded 9.8 seconds for 110 yards in competition. The Airlie Birds sold Terry Devonshire to York for a nominal fee on the eve of the match and were without the injured Alan McGlone

and honeymooning John Maloney. Roger Millward, Paul Longstaff and Brian Mennell were unavailable for the Robins, who had Terry Major and Alan Burwell injured and Frank Foster missing following appendicitis. But they welcomed John Taylor out of retirement.

Firth was initiated into derby rugby league in Hull with a nose injury, but he did score a try and it should have made the game safe for the Airlie Birds because it extended their lead to 20-8. At that point early in the second half Sullivan, Alf Macklin and Dick Gemmell had also touched down for Hull and Arthur Keegan and Arthur Keegan had kicked four goals. Tries by John Moore and Les Foster and a conversion by Bill Holliday had represented Rovers' only replies, but

Rovers scrum-half Colin Cooper kicks out at Hull's Shaun O'Brien in the incident that got them both sent off in the 1969 Eva Hardaker Memorial Trophy meeting.

they controlled the latter stages of the match and Moore's second try proved to the matchwinner. Phil Coupland also scored two tries for the Robins, Holliday landed two more goals and they sneaked home 21-20.

The 1969 Eva Hardaker Memorial Trophy meeting took place at Craven Park on July 30 and proved once and for all that the annual affair should be classified more as a charity match rather than a pre-season friendly – because two play-

Hull's Jim Macklin on the burst in the 1969 Hardaker game watched by Rovers' Alan Burwell.

Rovers' Phil Lowe and Hull's Joe Brown in a tangle in the 1970 Eva Hardaker Memorial Trophy game.

ers were sent off. The 5,500 crowd also saw Hull end a run of five successive defeats in the series in uncompromising style. They were without Terry Kirchin, their summer signing from Barrow, because of hamstring trouble, but they had Clive Sullivan back on the wing after a lengthy lay-off, while Terry Major returned to the Robins' line-up for his first appearance since breaking his arm the previous January.

The game exploded after 20 minutes when Hull's prop Shaun O'Brien and Rovers' scrum-half Colin Cooper were

Rovers' Max Rooms is injured in the 1970 clash.

Hull's Chris Davidson is stopped by Rovers' Cliff Wallis and Max Rooms in the 1970 meeting.

dismissed after a dust-up, but it was a sideline to the main action. Most of that came from the Airlie Birds, who led 19-2 at half-time and never looked back as they gave Rovers a 48-15 trouncing. Hull amassed ten tries from Roy Firth, Jim Macklin (two), Alf Macklin, Dick Gemmell, Clive Sullivan (two), Brian Hancock, Chris Davidson and Arthur Keegan, who also helped himself to nine goals, while Rovers had to be content with tries by Alan Burwell, Peter Small and Roger Millward, who kicked three goals. David Doyle-Davidson was the only Hull back not to touch down and it was too much for Rovers' chairman Wilf Spaven, who immediately called a board meeting to inquire into the gravity of the defeat. 'We were very disturbed about the result. It is beyond a joke when the other side get 48 points against us', he insisted. And it was a derby match, after all.

The 1970 meeting brought the only draw of the series when it ended 12-12.

For Hull, Howard Firth and Clive Sullivan scored tries, Joe Brown dropped a goal and Chris Davidson landed two goals, while Rovers' points came from tries by Ian Markham and Phil Lowe, who also suffered a serious shoulder injury, and three goals from Roger Millward.

Rovers returned to winning ways in 1971 in front of 4,500 fans at Craven Park on July 23 – the earliest that one of the matches was to be played. It was a new-look Craven Park because the main stand was being repainted in red and white, the terracing at the tote club corner was being relaid, new entrances were planned at the social club corner, there were new turnstiles and a new Press box and the bars had been repainted. The Robins gave a derby debut to former Sheffield rugby union centre George Kirkpatrick, but they were without forwards Phil Lowe and Gordon Young, while hooker Alan McGlone was fit to play for Hull after a hand injury.

As it was, the game's injury hoodoo struck again and McGlone was the victim because he was stretchered off with damaged knee ligaments to face a three-month absence. Rovers' Paul Rose also took a knock, but his side were already in the driving seat, having gone ahead with a third-minute try by Joe Brown, who had scored for Hull in the corresponding game only 11 months earlier. Terry Clawson landed three first-half goals to give the Robins a 9-3 lead with Hull's only reply coming from a try by Clive Sullivan. The Robins managed three more tries from Paul Daley (two) and Phil Coupland before Hull replied with a late try by Kenny Foulkes, to which John

Maloney added the goal, in a 20-8 defeat.

Hull might outwardly have looked as if they were in some disarray in the build-up to the 1972 game because team manager Roy Francis had been given a month's leave of absence, Johnny Whiteley was on holiday and Ivor Watts was in charge instead. In addition, Terry Devonshire and Nick Trotter were ruled out because of hamstring injuries. Rovers, though, also had their fair share of problems because Ted Barnard, David Hick, Colin Cooper, John Moore and Mike Stephenson were injured and Roger Millward and Paul Longstaff were unavailable. There was a crowd of only 2,800 for the game at the Boulevard on August 12, but the Airlie Birds took their chance to improve their record in the series with both hands.

Hull had won 48-15 in 1969 and, although they did not run in as many points in 1972, their winning margin was bigger. In fact, they set a record for their biggest winning margin over the old enemy ever. They were 12-2 ahead by half-time and went on the rampage in the second half with second-row forward Mick Crane taking the man-of-the-match award. In all, the Airlie Birds ran in nine tries from Clive Sullivan (two), Paul Ibbertson (two), Keith Boxall, Howard Firth, Brian Hancock, Ken Huxley and Crane. Boxall and Jim Harrison succumbed to the traditional injury jinx so that the goalkicking duties were shared: Boxall kicked four, went to hospital with a gashed mouth and handed over to Mick Kendle, who landed four of his own. It ended up 43-8 with Rovers' only reply coming from tries by George Kirkpatrick and substitute

Ged Dunn, a try-scorer for Rovers in the 1973 match.

winger Tony Hutchinson and a first-half penalty by David Hall. But the catalogue of injuries hit the Robins even harder because Terry Hudson, Paul Rose and former Hull pair Jim Neale and Joe Brown were all casualties. In fact, there was a view from the Rovers camp that the game should be played in mid-campaign because it threw up so many pre-season injuries.

As it was, the 1973 clash took place at Craven Park a year to the day after the last one and Hull, now a Second Division club, further improved their record in the series against their higher-division rivals. The gate was even lower than a year earlier – 2,316 – and Rovers were again depleted with Roger Millward, Phil Lowe and Terry Hudson all missing. Clive Sullivan had become Hull's player-coach and he welcomed back Brian Hancock after a long absence.

Bernard Watson beats Hull's Jim Macklin to score his first try for Rovers in the 1974 Eva Hardaker Memorial Trophy game.

The game boiled over into a free-for-all early in the second half as a reminder that rivalries had been officially resumed, but Hull had taken the initiative by then because they had established a 14-0 advantage by half-time. Sullivan and Nick Trotter crossed for tries and John Maloney kicked four goals before Rovers responded with a try by Ged Dunn. Maloney converted Sullivan's second try to put the Airlie Birds 19-3 ahead before the Robins came storming back. Substitute Phil Lowe touched down, Dunn scored his second try, audaciously beckoning Sullivan to catch him as he chased towards the line, and Bob Woodhead landed both conversions, but Hull still won 19-13.

The 1974 Eva Hardaker Memorial Trophy meeting produced another low crowd of 2,400 when it took place at the Boulevard on August 18. Clive Sullivan was not playing, but he had moved across the city to Rovers, where he was scheduled to link up with another rugby league great, Neil Fox, who had been signed on a free transfer from Wakefield Trinity in the close season and made his debut for his new club amid the derby atmosphere. Hull had also lost Mick Harrison, but David Doyle-Davidson was their new coach, Chris Davidson was their new captain and Ian Stenton and Steve Portz formed a new centre partnership.

One aspect of the proceedings had not changed, though, because there was the almost-ritual mass brawl in the second half and this time Wakefield referee Fred Lindop, who was later to take charge of a derby clash at Wembley, took firm action, sending off Rovers' Ged Dunn and Hull's substitute Alan Wardell. There had been doubts about the wisdom of signing Fox, but he landed six goals out of nine attempts and Davidson was off-target with seven out of nine. It proved to be the crucial difference between the sides because it gave the Robins a 24-13 victory. They scored four tries with David Hall grabbing two of them and newcomer Bernard Watson and substitute Ian Madley one each. Davidson touched down for one try to add to his two goals and Portz and Terry Devonshire were Hull's other try-scorers.

The 1975 clash in front of a 2,729 attendance at Craven Park on August 10 was a classic. And it came after a suggestion to switch the game, which had twice been postponed because of heavy rain eight years earlier, of course, to the relative cool of a Monday evening because of a heatwave had been rejected. As it was, Rovers' coach Arthur Bunting claimed afterwards that the game had gone ahead

Rovers' Alan Burwell beats Hull full-back Paul Hunter to score in the 1975 match.

Rovers' Ged Dunn is halted by Hull's Keith Barr in the 1976 Eva Hardaker Memorial Trophy derby.

in Sunday-afternoon conditions that were too hot for rugby league. If his side had lost, it might have measured eight on the Alex Ferguson scale in terms of sporting excuses! In fact, the Robins won after a dramatic finale. They were without David Hall, Mike Smith, Ian Madley and Phil Coupland because of injury, while Cliff Wallis wanted to return to amateur rugby, Paul Rose was in Australia and Neil Fox was unavailable. But they included John Cunningham, their close-season signing from Barrow, in their pack. Hull were without the injured Arthur Gibbons, Tony Geraghty, Chris Davidson, Nick Trotter and Alan Wardell, while Mick Kendle, Don Robson and Bill Ramsey were unavailable.

The game itself raised the temperatures even more because it was not decided until the final minute when Mike Hughes scored Rovers' match-winning try, to which Bernard Watson added the goal to give them a 28-25 victory. And there was even a sending-off between the try and the goal when York referee Gerry Kershaw dismissed Hull's Tony Banham for dissent. Rovers' other points came from tries by Clive Sullivan, Steve Hartley, Alan Burwell and Glyn Turner in the first half and another by Watson, a conversion by Turner and three goals from Cunningham. Hull, who made several substitutions in the heat to go 25-23 ahead with a second-half rally after having been 16-5 behind at one point, scored with tries by George Clark (two), Mick Crane, substitute Steve Lane and Banham, four goals from Keith Boxall and a first-half penalty by Crane. The injury toll was again impressive with Rovers losing Turner, Cunningham and Hartley and Hull winger Alf Macklin breaking his toe.

There were no more derby clashes until the next Eva Hardaker Memorial Trophy meeting at the Boulevard on August 8, 1976, when a slightly-better crowd of 3,214 saw another high-scoring thriller. Sadly, some of the younger rival fans clashed before the kick-off in a rare occurrence of derby unrest on the terraces. Hull coach David Doyle-Davidson reckoned that the previous year's meeting had been one of the best games in the history of the series and hoped for a repeat. He got it and the Airlie Birds, who were linked with Welsh international rugby union full-back John 'J. P. R.' Williams, won to keep up the two-year cycle of results that had developed. And Rovers' coach Harry Poole might have taught Ron Atkinson a thing or two – he was on holiday during the build-up to the game and turned up just in time to watch it!

Hull led 18-12 at half-time and, although Rovers cut their deficit to three points at one stage, there was not the same kind of grandstand finish as there had been a year earlier. The Airlie Birds were unruffled when they led 28-15 on another sweltering derby day and it was merely to the Robins' credit that they made the final scoreline of 28-23 look more respectable. The two No. 11s did most of the scoring because Keith Boxall scored two tries and kicked two goals to account for ten of Hull's points and Alan Ackroyd crossed for one try and landed four goals for a tally of 11 points for Rovers. Hull's other tries came from Malcolm Walker, who won the man-of-the-match award, Mervyn Hicks on his return to the club, Steve Portz and Brian Hancock, while George Robinson kicked three goals. Three of Rovers' other tries came from substitutes – two by Steve Hartley and one by Ray Norrie – while Terry Lynn touched down on only his second first-team appearance for the club. Hartley had replaced Ian Robinson, who had gone off with severe concussion after one of the more acrimonious incidents of the game.

The attendance again went up a little – to 3,600 – for the 1977 meeting in the competition on August 14 at Craven Park and there was no close finish this time because Rovers comfortably won 29-18. Ironically, the Robins were below-strength in the forwards and Hull were depleted in the backs with Keith Hepworth dropping out at the last minute.

Howard Firth, the young Riding rugby union player and a prolific scorer, who was the 'mystery trialist' in the 1968 Eva Hardaker derby.

Paul Prendiville, the 'mystery trialist' who made his debut in the 1978 Eva Hardaker derby.

Hull were reminded that they would need to consolidate in First Division rugby and their main consolation was that Keith Boxall crossed for a hat-trick of tries to add to the three that he had recently scored for Great Britain against Rovers. Loose-forward Mick Crane scored Hull's other try and David Marshall kicked three conversions as they bounced back from being 18-0 down at one point. But the Robins made light of being repeatedly penalised by Wakefield referee Ron Moore and ran in seven tries from man-of-the-match award winner Ian Robinson (two), Wally Youngman (two), Mike Hughes, John Millington and Mike Smith, while off-half David Hall kicked four goals.

There was another close, high-scoring encounter at the Boulevard on August 6,

1978, in front of yet another improved crowd of 4,492. Hull, now managed by Arthur Bunting, the former Rovers player and coach, were without forward Richard 'Charlie' Stone, signed for £15,000 from Featherstone Rovers in the summer, but Vince Farrar was back in the pack after a knee operation. The Robins included teenage forward Mark Davidson in their starting line-up and Phil Lowe, fresh from an arm operation, in the centre. But the main interest surrounded two former rugby union players because Hull opted for a trialist full-back and Rovers gave a debut to former Hull and East Riding and Marist winger Garry McHugh. In 1968 many fans knew the identity of Hull's so-called mystery trialist Howard Firth: this time there was more intrigue involved, but he turned out to be 24-year-old Paul Prendiville, from Llanelli, who had been a prolific scorer for West Wales League side Bynea.

Prendiville made his mark at full-back in the Eva Hardaker Memorial Trophy with five goals from seven attempts on his debut and within a week Hull had completed his change of codes. Hull, who led 21-8 at one stage, also ran in six tries from Ian Wilson (two), Keith Barr, Ian Crowther, new centre Chris Harrison and Mick Sutton. Rovers, who had twice been in the lead with tries by Lowe and John Cunningham and a conversion by David Hall, rallied late on to make the scoreline look more respectable. Coach Roger Millward made an amazing 11 substitutions at various points, but further points came from tries by Hall, Cunningham again, Ian Robinson and Ged Dunn and two conversions by Allan Agar although the Airlie Birds held on for a 28-24 triumph.

The next derby meeting was to be the final match in the Eva Hardaker Memorial Trophy series. It was another high-scoring affair, it brought Hull another win and it was watched by an even better crowd of 5,005. It took place on August 5, 1979, and was a clash between the Rugby League champions Rovers and the Second Division champions Hull, but the sides were seriously depleted. The Airlie Birds were without the injured Graham Bray, Steve Norton and 'Charlie' Stone were on tour and Keith Tindall, 'Sammy' LLoyd and Graham Evans were unavailable, but Keith Hepworth was on the substitutes' bench after a recent cartilage operation. The tour of Australasia also weakened the Robins, whose player-coach Roger Millward had just had a cartilage operation in Sydney, while Phil Lowe, Paul Rose, Clive Sullivan and Ian Madley were all injured.

Colin Lazenby, who had once been a winger with Rovers' Colts, proved to be the match-winner as a prop with Hull because he helped himself to 15 points with a try and six goals. Alf Macklin, Chris Harrison, Clive Pickerill and Keith Boxall were the Airlie Birds' other try-scorers. Rovers' tries came from Steve Hartley (two), David Hall and substitute Steve Leighton, while Steve Hubbard and Ian Robinson both landed two conversions. It was a game of cut and thrust as the lead changed hands with Hull 12-10 ahead at half-time, before settling for a 27-20 win. And in the closing stages the series of pre-season charity matches ended on a typically-quirky note because Hull ended up with 15 players on the pitch at one point amid the various substitutions and referee Fred Lindop awarded Rovers a penalty as a result of the numerical indiscretion!

Above: Hull winger Norman Oliver is stopped during a derby in April 1966.

Previous page, top: Rovers' Mike Blackmore, who was later sent off, is hauled down by Hull's Ken Foulkes (left) and Brian Sullivan in April 1965.

Previous page, bottom: Rovers loose-forward Harry Poole searches for support in April 1965.

Left: Rovers' David Elliott touches down in April 1966.

Rovers' David Elliott touches down for one of his tries in a derby in April 1966.

Rovers' Terry Major stops Hull winger Norman Oliver in April 1966.

Rovers' Chris Young beats Hull's Geoff Stocks and John Maloney to score in April 1966.

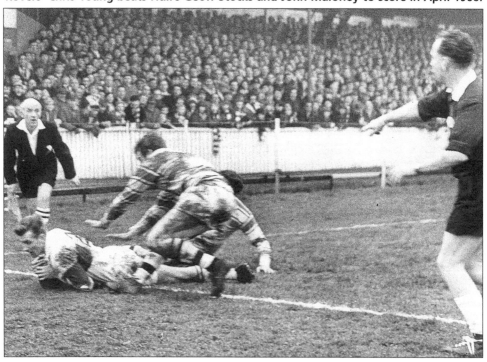

Final Countdowns

I T WAS always to be expected that everything was at stake when Hull FC and Hull Kingston Rovers clashed in rugby league derbies. The majority of games might be in the league and might, when all was said and done, have just two points split one of three ways as the end-product. You could, of course, win a league one season and lose the derby games: that was the greater consolation for the league champions. There again, the derby winners may not have any silverware in the cupboard, but they might always boast that they won the games that really mattered. They might even claim a little outrageously that they were the 'unofficial' champions because they had beaten the side who were the 'official' champions on the accepted points basis.

It was very different with cup-ties, though. You could win a major cup competition by succeeding in just a few games and you did not have to go through the rigmarole of playing well week in and week out during a league campaign to pull of a significant achievement. But the one-off nature of a cup-tie does add an extra tasty ingredient simply because there is not the possibility of honours being even and the points being shared. Someone had to lose and go out of what would often be a money-spinning tournament until the next season. The compensation of losing a derby and winning the league was not part of the

equation any more, so defeat would be even more unpallatable than usual. And the luck of the draw for the competition meant that Hull and Rovers would frequently find themselves lining up against one another with even more at stake than ever. It was, of course, the reason why cup competitions exist in any sport in the first place because the sudden-death aspect of the occasion make them even more unbearable for some.

The first cup meeting between Hull and Rovers was the seventh derby of all on March 2, 1902. It was a 15-a-side game, which attracted a 10,000 gate to Craven Park on a sunny day, in the second round of the Northern Union Cup and both sides had yet to concede a point in the competition. Hull, who were then in the Northern Rugby League and had previously had a poor cup record, chose the same squad of players who had beaten York, then known as the Eborites, 28-0 in the first round in which Rovers, then in the Lancashire Senior Competition, had defeated St Helen's 7-0. They brought in former Cardiff player McConnell and Taylor. And because it was the first senior cup-tie derby the game was described at the time as 'a landmark in the history of local football'.

Rovers soon took a 5-0 lead with a goal by Smith and a try by Jim Barry, but even though they were the more dominant side in early stages, it was to be the end of their scoring. And Hull reduced the arrears initially with a drop goal by Billy Jacques to make it 5-2 at half-time. 'Fatty' Thompson took a painful knock early in the second half, but he then played a part in sending in Parry in the corner. As Hull took command, Parry scored his second try and then Parkinson made it 11-5 with a penalty following a scrum infringement. That proved to be the end of the scoring and Hull went through to the third round in which they were beaten 13-2 away to the then powerful Broughton Rangers. The breakdown of the electric tram service then caused congestion after a derby in which it was reported: 'The tackling was of a severe character and it was no wonder that the injuries were frequent.' It had set the trend for derby cup-ties.

The score was almost the same in the next derby cup-tie, which took place in the second round of the Yorkshire Cup on October 31, 1914, and attracted a 14,000 crowd. The weather had been extremely wet in the build-up to the match and the military curtain-raiser was called off as a precaution. The game also took place against the backcloth of the so-called Great War and news filtered through before the kick-off of the death of former Rovers forward Brain after he had been shot in the shoulder in combat with the West Yorkshire Regiment. In addition, Arthur Moore, who was later to lead the Robins when they won the Yorkshire Cup for the first time, was in the crowd with his arm in a sling after being discharged from a military hospital. Hull, who had had a first-round bye, were without their suspended hero Billy Batten, snr., while Rovers had already beaten Wakefield Trinity 10-5 at home in

the competition. And both sides had by then been beaten Yorkshire Cup finalists – Rovers having gone down 8-5 to Bradford at Wakefield in the 1906-07 final and Hull having been defeated 17-3 by Batley at Leeds in the 1912-13 final.

Rovers soon seized the initiative and took a deserved 16th-minute lead with a penalty by Alf Carmichael. Four minutes later Vaughan went over for a try after a kick had been charged down, but, just as they had done 12 years earlier, the Robins threw away a 5-0 advantage and never scored again. Back came Hull with winger Jack Harrison scoring his 18th try of the season to maintain his record of averaging one a match and that was how it stayed until the final quarter of the match. Centre Jimmy Devereux then sold a dummy to score a try that nudged Hull 6-5 in front and then literally went to great pains to secure victory in the last minute. He broke a bone in his right forearm as he sent in Hull's other winger Alf Francis before Ned Rogers added the conversion to give Hull an 11-5 triumph. They then took revenge over Batley by beating them 7-0 in the semi-finals before again losing in the final when Huddersfield trounced them 31-0 at Leeds.

The last derby to be played at Craven Street before Rovers moved to the original Craven Park was the next cup-tie between the two clubs and it took place in the second round of the Rugby League Challenge Cup on March 11, 1922. The ground was packed to the rafters with an 18,000 crowd and it was apt that the referee, Pendleton's Albert Hestford, was regarded as one of the top officials in the game. Hull, for whom Eddie Caswell and

Bob Taylor passed late fitness tests, had been runners-up in the league the previous season and had beaten Halifax 24-10 at home in the first round. Rovers, who had won 4-2 at York in the first round, had been the champions, so there was plenty at stake.

The match was a typically tight affair and there was no scoring until the 67th minute when, ironically, Caswell and Taylor combined to break the deadlock. Taylor, described as 'a man and a half with a penchant for wildness', touched down although there was a suspicion that Caswell's pass to him had been forward and then Jim Kennedy clinched a 10-0 victory for Hull with a further try and goal as they made the most of their limited chances. And Hull went nearly all the way in the Challenge Cup that season, winning 9-4 at Dewsbury in the third round and beating Wigan 18-5 in the semi-finals at Leeds, where they agonisingly went down 10-9 to Rochdale Hornets in the final.

Later the same year the first derby cup-tie at Craven Park took place when Hull and Rovers met in the first round of the Yorkshire Cup. There was a 21,000 crowd on October 21, 1922, as the Robins strove to end a run of ten successive home defeats against the Airlie Birds. And it came exactly a fortnight after the first derby at Craven Park when Hull had won 10-7, but this time Rovers were finally to end their jinx. The Robins brought back Arthur Moore in place of George van Rooyen, while Hull's Welsh international Fred Samuel was unavailable although they brought back Bob Taylor and Tom Milner. And improvements had been made to Craven Park in the intervening two weeks because crush barriers had been installed at the entrance to the turnstiles, there was additional banking and the road into the ground had been repaired.

Rovers repeatedly ploughed their way through the middle and that was how winger Louis Harris scored their first try after just two minutes. Laurie Osborne added the conversion and landed another goal after seven minutes before Jim Kennedy made it 7-2 at half-time when he reduced the deficit with another kick. Osborne put the Robins 9-2 ahead with a second-half drop goal from almost on the halfway line and he completed the scoring for a 14-2 success with another conversion after Rees had touched down under the posts in the closing stages. The Robins made no further progress in the competition, however, because they lost 15-3 at Batley in the second round.

Later in the same season there was another derby that underlined the incongruity of rugby league thinking. It took place at the Boulevard on April 21, 1923, in the Rugby League Championships play-off semi-finals. Hull had finished at the top of the league, but then the top four played off and they met Rovers, who had finished fourth, with Huddersfield and Swinton meeting in the other game. The Robins went on to defeat Huddersfield 15-5 in the final at Leeds, so who were the real champions in everyone's eyes? Both clubs could at least claim to have had memorable seasons and it meant that this game was trumpeted as 'the derby of derbies' although some fascinating contests between the old rivals had already started to develop. Certainly something had to give on this occasion because Hull had won 13 games in a row and Rovers had just recorded eight successive victories. There were high hopes, too, that the gate receipts would top the £1,500 mark with half each going to the two clubs minus incidental expenses. Veteran referee Frank Renton, from Hunslet, was in charge of the game, having first controlled a derby clash in 1904, and it attracted an attendance of 28,000.

Hull were soon handicapped by knocks to Billy Batten, snr., and Ned Rogers, who was hurt when he tried in vain to stop Gilbert Austin from scoring Rovers' first try in the corner. Jack Hoult then scored under the posts and Laurie Osborne's conversion made it 8-0 after half an hour. In the second half Billy Westerdale and Austin added further tries and Osborne landed another goal, while Hull's only points again came from a penalty by Jim Kennedy as they went down 16-2. But while Rovers went on to win the play-off final, the season brought more anti-climax for Hull because they were then well-beaten 28-3 by Leeds at Wakefield in the final of the Rugby League Challenge Cup.

The next cup-tie derby was not until September 12, 1936, when Hull and Rovers again met in the first round of the Yorkshire Cup. The game attracted a 15,000 crowd and also featured a junior derby between Craven Park Juniors and Boulevard Old Boys as a curtain-raiser. There was also a reminder to the public that the Rugby League's cup-tie regulations meant that there would be no reduced admission prices to the seniors' clash for the unemployed. As it was, Hull

had won six and drawn one of the last seven derbies and were the favourites as the current rugby league champions, but they were given a harder battle than they might have anticipated. They brought in George Mathers at loose-forward, while Rovers recalled Harry Beaumont and John Eastwood.

Joe Oliver soon gave Hull the lead with a try and a goal, but Victor Young touched down for Rovers and Wilf McWatt made it 5-5. It set the pattern for the game because Billy Stead restored Hull's lead with Oliver tacking on the conversion. But then McWatt landed a penalty for Rovers, who drew level at 10-10 by half-time thanks to 'Bunker' Wood's try. George Barlow's try put Hull back in front, but Young's solo effort 15 minutes from time made it 13-13. McWatt, though, missed the kick in front of the posts and the salt was poured into Rovers' wounds when Oliver then kicked two match-winning penalties on a day on which they had generally committed too many infringements. The Airlie Birds won 17-13 and then beat Leeds 12-9 in the second round before losing 5-0 at York at the semi-final stage.

Rovers earned their cup-tie revenge over Hull on February 4, 1939, with another closely-fought derby in the first round of the Rugby League Challenge Cup in front of a 22,000 crowd, who paid record ground receipts of £1,349, at Craven Park. Hull had been beaten 18-10 by Huddersfield at Bradford in the Yorkshire Cup final earlier in the season, but Rovers had won five successive home games. And a new bus service catered for supporters from North Hull, setting off from Endike Lane via Clough Road,

Stoneferry, Chamberlain Road, Laburnum Avenue and Holderness Road, while extra trams were put on from the city centre.

Jack Dawson, described as '15 stones of hurtling speed', opened the scoring with a try for Hull, but Rovers responded with a try by Lou Beaumont and a conversion by Wilf McWatt to go 5-3 in front. Joe Oliver, by now in the Robins' ranks, was caught offside to give Freddie Miller the chance to equalise with a penalty. They had to withstand some heavy pressure in the second half, but a sweet passing movement sent centre Jack Spamer through a narrow gap for the winning try and Hull had gone down 8-5. Rovers did not progress any further in the competition, though, because they lost 6-2 at Halifax in the second round.

The first post-war cup-tie derby was a semi-final sizzler and produced a piece of rugby league history when a crowd of 17,034 went to the Boulevard on October 10, 1946, for a Yorkshire Cup clash. It was the first all-ticket rugby league match ever and produced receipts of £1,512 in addition to a seesaw struggle. The Yorkshire Cup's first round was over two legs at that time, so both clubs had played three games on their way to the semi-finals. Hull had beaten Featherstone Rovers 16-10 and 24-3 in the first round before overcoming York 42-8 at the Boulevard, while Rovers had defeated Halifax 10-9 and 11-7 before winning 15-10 at Huddersfield. They were at full strength after clearing up injury doubts about Joe Ramsden, Emlyn Richards and Wilf McWatt.

Richards travelled to the game from Birmingham on the morning of the match, but it did not prevent him from giving Rovers the lead when he went over in the corner. Freddie Miller reduced the arrears with a penalty for Hull, but the Robins were 11-2 ahead early in the second half after further tries by Richards and Ronnie Mills and a goal by McWatt. But then it all turned sour for them as the Airlie Birds mounted a sterling comeback with tries by Ivor Watts (two) and Ernie Lawrence and a further two goals from Miller to win 15-11. Hull went on to face Wakefield in the final, but went down 10-0 at Leeds.

Rovers came up against Hull's 'great pack' in the next cup-tie derby when 24,000 packed into the Boulevard on March 21, 1959. It was in the third round of the Rugby League Challenge Cup and the Airlie Birds really were on their way to Wembley. They had already beaten Blackpool Borough 11-2 and Wakefield Trinity 16-10 in a replay after a 4-4 draw at the Boulevard, while the Robins had accounted for Widnes 3-2 and Castleford 20-0 in two home ties. Hull were without injured full-back Arthur Keegan and former Halifax rugby union centre Brian Saville because he was needed for an Army game, while Peter Key had recovered from illness to take his place in the centre for Rovers, who gave derby debuts to Graham Paul and Alvin Ackerley, leading to a confrontation between two of the game's top hookers as he opposed Tommy Harris.

The two full-backs, Hull's Peter Bateson and Rovers' Cyril Kellett, exchanged early penalties in a close first half. Johnny Whiteley then scored the first try of the day for Hull before Kellett landed a further penalty to make it 5-4 at the interval. In the second half, though, the Airlie Birds went on the rampage as they established an unassailable 23-4 lead. Dick Boustead, who had been limping earlier, ran in two tries, Jim Drake, who had to go off near the end with blood running down his face, added another and Johnny Whiteley touched down for a second time, while Bateson chipped in with a penalty and two conversions. The Robins, hampered by a second-half ankle injury to David Elliott, could manage only a late consolation try from winger Brian Coulson, to which Kellett tacked on the conversion. Hull got through 23-9 and then beat Featherstone Rovers 15-5 at Odsal in their first appearance in the semi-finals since 1935, but they went down 30-13 to Wigan in the final at Wembley.

Two seasons later Hull and Rovers met in another Rugby League Challenge Cup clash. It took place in the second round in front of a 17,000 gate at the Boulevard and Hull's coach Roy Francis summed up the demands of a cup-tie derby when he said beforehand: "One of the nice things about about a cup-tie – in particular, a Hull v Rovers tie – is that some official prophet is going to be wrong. It might be Wilf Spaven, Ernest Hardaker, Colin Hutton or myself and two of the four are going to be crying into their best bitter. Not being over-fond of watered-down beer, I hope it is Wilf and Colin! While I am all for brotherly love, share and share alike and new faces at Wembley, those of Hull Kingston Rovers are the ones I do not want to see there this year." The Airlie Birds, who had beaten Oldham 4-2 at home in the first round, left out Gordon Harrison

and Brian Hambling, while the Robins, who had had a comfortable first-round passage when they beat amateurs Pilkington Rec. 56-8 in the first round, gave a derby debut to Harry Poole at loose-forward and otherwise went for youth. They fielded a side with an average of 22 after omitting Ken Kingsbury, Bill Riley and Alvin Ackerley.

There was little between the two sides in the first half on a quagmire of a pitch after continuous rain, but Hull led 2-0 thanks to a penalty by Peter Bateson. There was no further score until ten minutes into the second half when Tommy Harris twice set up tries, first for Tommy Finn and then for Jim Drake. Bateson tacked on the conversions and two penalties and all that the Robins had to show for their efforts was an obstruction try awarded to Graham Paul. Hull went through 16-3 and then sneaked home 10-9 against Featherstone Rovers at the Boulevard, but their hopes of a third consecutive trip to Wembley were dashed in the semi-finals when they were beaten 26-9 by St Helen's at Odsal.

The first Yorkshire Cup tie between Hull and Rovers for almost 20 years took place at the Boulevard on September 3, 1966. And it was to prove a bit special because the crowd of 8,302 saw a first-round clash which was to boast the highest aggregate of points for any derby cup-tie. Hull had recent signing Ron Morgan back after knee trouble, but Eric Broom, Alan McGlone, Terry Devonshire and Jim Neale were ruled out by injuries, while Kenny Foulkes returned at scrum-half with David Doyle-Davidson switching to centre in Joe Brown's place. Rovers, winners of 12

Mike Blackmore scored two tries in the first Yorkshire Cup tie between Hull and Rovers for almost 20 years at the Boulevard in September 1966.

Hull's Mick Harrison is brought down by a combination of Rovers' Frank Fox, Frank Foster and Bill Holliday in the Yorkshire Cup in September 1966.

out of the previous 14 derby clashes, included Alan Burwell, who had just made a surprise comeback, but although Roger Millward, Terry Major and Frank Foster passed late fitness checks, David Elliott was ruled out by injury.

Hull's John Maloney and Rovers' Cyril Kellett exchanged early penalties, but then came the first surge of superiority. It came from the Airlie Birds, who led 10-2 after tries by Norman Oliver and Ken Owens and a conversion by Maloney. But back stormed the Robins, who led 17-10 by the interval as John Moore and Mike Blackmore (two) touched down for tries and Kellett added on two conversions and a penalty. Doyle-Davidson scored another try for Hull and Maloney converted it before landing a 35-yard penalty to level the scores at 17-17, but then Rovers regained command again, initially with another penalty by Kellett. Arthur Bunting then weaved his way through from the base of a scrum to score a vital try and Kellett's conversion

made it 24-17. But Hull refused to give in and Clive Sullivan crossed for a try that set up a tense finale in what was regarded as one of the most absorbing derbies ever. Rovers got home 24-20 and were never tested as sternly again as they went on to win the Yorkshire Cup. They won 29-3 at Hunslet and beat Huddersfield 27-7 at home before overcoming Featherstone Rovers 25-12 at Headingley in the final.

The two sides met again in the Yorkshire Cup's first round on August 28, 1970, but this time Hull won comfortably at Craven Park. The game attracted a crowd of 7,337 and took place against a backcloth of upheaval in both camps, particularly the rumours that two of the city's all-time rugby league

Rovers' winger Chris Young is caught by Hull's Clive Sullivan during the Yorkshire Cup clash in September 1966.

heroes, Hull's Clive Sullivan and Rovers' Roger Millward, wanted transfers. Both played, though, but the Airlie Birds were also without Joe Brown, who was embroiled in a pay dispute with them although the official line was that he was

Hull elation as Ken Owens celebrates his try in a Yorkshire Cup clash in September 1966. Ken Foulkes retrieves the ball while Rovers' Brian Tyson turns away.

excluded because he missed training, and Arthur Keegan, who had a broken arm. Millward and Peter 'Flash' Flanagan were passed fit after late tests, but Geoff Wriglesworth was missing, so Ron Willett, recently signed from Castleford, made his debut in a derby for Rovers, who also snapped up local forward Ray Cardy during the build-up to the game.

Hull might also have had worries about a successor to ace goalkicker John Maloney, but forward Keith Boxall made his mark with six goals from six attempts and Sullivan, playing in the centre, was at his mercurial best with three tries in ten first-half minutes. Howard Firth also touched down before the interval when the Airlie Birds led 18-4. The Robins, handicapped by first-half injuries to Ian Markham and Gordon Young, managed a second-half try, scored by Willett on his debut, and Terry Clawson landed a conversion and two penalties. But the irrepressible Sullivan set up a try for loose-forward Paul Ibbertson and Hull cantered home 27-9. They then hammered Doncaster 42-0 in the second round before agonisingly succumbing 12-11 to Leeds at Headingley at the semi-final stage.

The following season it was back to Rugby League Challenge Cup duties with a first-round derby that had to be postponed three times in a week before it finally went ahead in front of a 7,100 crowd at the Boulevard on February 3, 1972, after a thaw. Another problem at one point was the possibility of a power cut, but none materialised and the two teams were as originally selected. The next hazard was the torrential rain throughout the first half that threatened

an abandonment at one stage, but it eventually eased and the game was completed at long last.

Hull crafted a breakthrough after 15 minutes when Brian Hancock raced on to his own kick to touch down and Keith Boxall tacked on the goal to make it 5-0. But Rovers drew level in the second half with a penalty by Roger Millward and a try in the corner by Mike Stephenson. The decisive moment, though, came midway through the second half when Rovers' Jim Neale, facing his old club, flattened Nick Trotter with a high tackle and Boxall knocked over the match-winning penalty. Millward missed a difficult last-minute penalty that would have forced a replay, so Hull went through 7-5 before losing 16-5 to Leeds at the Boulevard in the second round.

Exactly two years later – on February 3, 1974 – the two sides again met at the Boulevard at the same stage of the same competition, but this time the result was very different. After all, Rovers were in the First Division and Hull were in the Second Division in the first season since the one-division format had been abandoned. Barry Kear made his derby debut for Hull, who were in the throes of a backroom row with former director David Bassett, after they had pipped Rovers for his signature. The Robins were close to full strength after Paul Rose had recovered from injury, but Roger Millward was forced to drop out at the last minute on doctor's orders.

It turned out to be a rough derby as Rovers set out to take control from the outset, going ahead with a 14th-minute try by half-back Mike Stephenson, who touched down despite being tripped just

Hull full-back Tony Geraghty is stopped by Rovers' scrum-half Terry Hudson in the RL Challenge Cup derby in February 1974.

short of the line. Hull scrum-half Chris Davidson reduced the arrears with a penalty four minutes later, but John Millington and John Moore touched down for further tries for the Robins before the interval when it was 11-2 after David Hall had converted one of them. It was not until six minutes from time that scrum-half Terry Hudson added to Rovers' lead with a drop goal, but soon afterwards the game finally boiled over. Four separate fights ensued after an initial incident involving Millington and Hull duo Len Casey and Alan McGlone. The upshot was that try-scorer Millington and Hull substitute Alan Wardell were dismissed by Oldham referee Sam Shepherd as Rovers won 13-2 before going down 12-9 at home to

Featherstone Rovers in the second round.

The next derby cup-tie was in the second round of the Rugby League Challenge Cup on February 26, 1977, when 10,939 fans packed into Craven Park for another game played when the two sides were in separate divisions. This time, though, Hull, 34-11 winners at home to Doncaster in the first round, were well on their way to the Second Division title although they were without influential scrum-half Keith Hepworth because of a groin injury. Rovers, whose coach Harry Poole was to die tragically young a month later, brought in Mike Hughes for the suspended Roy Holdstock, while teenage centre Mike Smith was ruled fit after hamstring trouble. They had beaten Keighley 20-10 at home in the first round.

A section of the crowd spilled over on to the greyhound track when a perimeter fence collapsed just before the kick-off and there was little to choose between the two sides for long periods. Early in the second half it was 6-6 after the two full-backs, Rovers' Colin Tyrer and Hull's David Marshall, had both landed three penalties as Salford referee Peter Massey clamped down at the first sign of any indiscretion. But Phil Lowe supplied the turning-point with the first try of the match for the Robins 15 minutes from time as he charged over with three Hull players hanging on to him and Tyrer added the conversion. Roger Millward dropped a goal to make it 12-6 to Rovers and it finished 12-9 after Brian Hancock

Phil Lowe provided the turning-point of the RL Challenge Cup second-round match at Craven Park in February 1977.

All eyes on a high kick in a cup derby in February 1977.

Hull's Brian Hancock scores a cup-tie try after beating Rovers' Ged Dunn and Steve Hartley in February 1977.

had finally broken through to touch down for the Airlie Birds. The Robins, for whom Smith and Paul Rose battled on with injuries, then won 25-15 at Castleford before going down 14-5 to Widnes at Headingley in the semi-finals.

Exactly a year later – on February 26, 1978 – the two sides clashed again in the same competition, but this time it was at the first-round stage and both were in the First Division by then. There was an attendance of 16,001 at the Boulevard to see a Hull side strengthened by two top-class forward acquisitions, Vince Farrar and Steve 'Knocker' Norton, who were making their derby debuts.

It was to be an explosive occasion with Widnes referee Ron Campbell sending off Rovers duo Phil Lowe and Colin Tyrer in the second half. He had already upset the Robins' camp earlier in the sea-son by dismissing Steve Hartley and Clive Sullivan for the first time in their careers in a John Player Trophy tie at Featherstone. They had lost 25-24 then and again it did not prevent the tie from being an extremely close affair because 11-man Rovers' resolve was not broken until the last minute when winger Alf Macklin grabbed Hull's match-winning try. Tyrer and Keith Boxall had earlier exchanged penalties before the Robins, also handicapped by a shoulder injury to David Watkinson, went ahead with a try by Sullivan. Tyrer's conversion hit the woodwork and Boxall then made it 5-4 with his second penalty. Tyrer and Boxall again exchanged penalties before Macklin clinched victory, Boxall missing the conversion after Rovers fans had thrown a number of objects on to the pitch in their anger. Hull made no further progress in the competition, though, because Widnes beat them 20-8 at the Boulevard in the second round.

On September 15, 1985, the two clubs clashed in the Yorkshire Cup's first round at Craven Park in front of a crowd of 10,116 and again there were just two points in it. Hull, who had won the trophy for the previous three seasons, were without Steve Norton, but Fred Ah Kuoi returned from injury and recent signing Andy Gascoigne partnered him at half-back on his derby debut. Gavin Miller, David Watkinson and Phil Hogan all came through late fitness tests for Rovers.

Hogan was to be a major influence as Hull moved into a 10-4 lead after 54 minutes. Dane O'Hara gave them a 4-0 lead with a 23rd-minute try, but Hogan made it 4-4 when he touched down 13 minutes later. Ah Kuoi and James Leuluai set up the Airlie Birds' second try, to which Gary Divorty added the conversion, but then the Robins bounced back, initially with John Dorahy landing a 62nd-minute penalty. Eleven minutes later Hogan took Miller's pass for his second try to leave it 10-10 and Dorahy's angled conversion saw Rovers home at 12-10. But there were after-match controversies with Hull's teenage forward Andy Dannatt wanting to know why he had been dropped and Rovers' Paul Harkin unhappy about being substituted at half-time. Rovers, meanwhile, went on to win the trophy that year, defeating Castleford 22-18 in the final at Headingley.

The next cup-tie derby was also at Craven Park and it attracted 8,746 fans for the first round of the Rugby League

Rovers' loose-forward Len Casey is stopped as Hull's Keith Boxall (left) and Mick Crane watch closely in the RL Challenge Cup derby in February 1977.

Challenge Cup on February 8, 1986. It was also the first derby in the competition since the all-Hull final at Wembley in 1980. Hull were beginning to get a settled side together under new team manager Kenny Foulkes, while Garry Clark, Gavin Miller and Phil Hogan all passed late fitness tests for Rovers, who had forward Chris Burton suspended.

Hull's Fred Ah Kuoi lasted just nine minutes before damaging a shoulder, while Burton's deputy, Des Harrison, broke his arm after just 27 minutes, but Rovers made light of the setback and John Dorahy emerged as their hero in a one-sided match, kicking five goals from six attempts and having a hand in his side's three tries as they built up a 16-0 lead after 48 minutes. Miller and substitute Andy Kelly had crossed for tries by then and nine minutes from time Mike Smith touched down for their third try. It was not until five minutes from the end that Hull earned any reward when Dane O'Hara scored a consolation try for them and Lee Crooks added the conversion. Rovers went through 22-6 in what was to become a dramatic cup run for them. They were forced to play two semi-finals at Elland Road, drawing 24-24 with Leeds the first time before defeating them 17-0 in the replay. They then lost 15-14 to Castleford in the final at Wembley.

And on September 13, 1992, there was to be another Yorkshire Cup first-round derby before the competition's demise. It took place in front of a gate of 8,825 at the Boulevard just after Hull had been pipped by Bradford Northern in a bold attempt to sign Great Britain scrum-half Deryck Fox from Featherstone Rovers.

Des Harrison suffered a broken arm after only 27 minutes of the February 1986 RL Challenge Cup match at Craven Park.

John Dorahy emerged as Rovers' hero in a one-sided RL Challenge Cup match in February 1986.

Hull prop Mike Harrison is halted by Rovers' Frank Fox (left) and Brian Tyson in March 1967.

Youngsters invade the Boulevard pitch after Hull's 13-12 win over Rovers in March 1967.

Rovers welcomed back forward Paul Fletcher after an elbow operation, but were without Craig O'Brien, who dropped out with a hamstring problem, Des Harrison and Wayne Jackson.

Hull's Paul Eastwood and Rovers' Mike Fletcher exchanged penalties in the opening 18 minutes and it was not until five minutes before the interval that there was any further score. Hull half-back Scott Gale kicked through to score on the sixth tackle and Eastwood's conversion made it 8-2, but two minutes into the second half Bright Sodje, whose brother Efe has played League soccer for Macclesfield Town, touched down for Rovers. Eastwood made it 10-6 with a 50th-minute penalty for obstruction, the Robins had centre Mike Bibby carried off with an ankle injury and then in the final minute the Airlie Birds secured their passage with a try by substitute Paul Harrison. They followed up their 14-6 triumph with a 26-16 win over Leeds at the Boulevard before losing 12-8 away to Sheffield Eagles at the semi-finals stage.

Rovers' full-back David Wainwright is halted by Hull's Norman Oliver in March 1967.

Rovers' Colin Cooper is buried under a group of Hull tacklers in March 1967.

Rovers' Bill Holliday (left) and Chris Young halt Hull's John Maloney in April 1967.

Floodlit Flings

IT IS a touch too trite and simplistic to come out with the simple statement that the majority of rugby league derbies between Hull FC and Hull Kingston Rovers during the course of a century have unfolded in daylight. Fans of any losing side who had gone down by a narrow margin could genuinely claim that they might have been the victims of 'daylight robbery'. But it does still have to be remembered that floodlights are a comparatively modern commodity. And once they had become a regular feature at rugby league grounds, it doubtless became a natural progression to invent a new competition designed especially to take place under lights. It happened when the BBC and the Rugby League got together to produce a cup competition played exclusively under lights. The ties were to be shown on BBC2 and it meant that the code was given a fresh opportunity to woo a wider audience.

It was within this framework that the BBC2 Floodlit Trophy was nurtured and Hull and Rovers met on three occasions in it as the traditional derby atmosphere became swathed in the warm glow that always seems to brighten up cold winter nights. And even though the three meetings were spread over a 12-year period, they did, in effect, provide a kind of final countdown of their own. That was because they took place in the preliminary round, the second round and then the final itself. In fact, it was the last final of all, so the winners were destined, in theory at least, to retain the trophy in perpetuity.

The first clash took place at Craven Park on September 18, 1967, and was one of six meetings between the sides that year. Hull won the first game in the league 13-12 and then went on to be beaten in the next five. The BBC2 Floodlit Trophy tie, though, attracted the second-highest gate of the six encounters and was bettered only by the Yorkshire Cup final derby tie a month later. That backcloth had further spice to the proceedings, of course, and the fact that an attendance of 14,280 attended the game in person to soak up its natural atmosphere when they might have settled for the comfort of being armchair TV fans that night speaks volumes for the importance of derby games in local eyes. And they produced what were then record gate receipts of £2,568 for a derby clash at Craven Park.

From the Robins' point of view, there were two other aspects of the game that added further interest to it. The club had been involved in a race against time to complete the installation of their new floodlights for the clash. As it was, the work on the £16,000 floodlights, comprising 192 lamps on four 110ft pylons, was completed the day before the match. There was another factor that affected Rovers' build-up because 24 hours before the game the club's chairman Wilf Spaven admitted that Leeds had made what was regarded as a sensational offer for their star forwards Bill Holliday and Frank Foster, offering them £14,000 plus stand-off half Mike Shoebottom in exchange. Curiously describing the offer as having been made 'casually', Mr Spaven insisted: 'In our opinion our players are worth a lot more than that. This offer may have been a feeler, but Leeds were told in no uncertain manner that we do not want to sell.' And he added, for good measure, that Rovers already had players who were as good as Shoebottom, if not better.

Holliday instead featured in the Robins' line-up for the derby although Foster was sidelined with a hand injury, Colin Cooper, Cyril Kellett, David Elliott and Peter Flanagan returned to the squad and Chris Young, Phil Lowe and Terry Major were available after passing fitness tests. Major, in fact, had been the subject of an offer from Leeds himself earlier that year after he had been transfer-listed, but the clubs failed to agree on

a fee. Hull, for their part, were without forwards Eric Broom and Jim Neale, but they were on form and were fourth in the league table – just one place ahead of Rovers.

The Airlie Birds starved Rovers of possession for long periods and soon led 2-0 with a penalty from John Maloney's sure boot. Kellett struck the upright with one of two penalty misses at the other end before the Robins went ahead when Phil Lowe touched down after Hull had lost possession from a scrum near their own line. And then Roger Millward, who was replaced at half-time by substitute Elliott after falling victim to a tackle that earned David Doyle-Davidson a caution, sent in Cooper in the corner for Rovers' second try. In fact, the captains were at one point called together to try to exert a calming influence on their colleagues. The Airlie Birds, meanwhile, were back in the game by the interval when winger Norman Oliver went over for their opening try to make it 6-5. Kellett finally kicked a penalty to nudge the Robins 8-5 in front before Hull dramatically hit back. Chris Davidson charged down a drop-out from Holliday and raced in for a try that brought the scores level, leaving Rovers to ponder the possibility of a replay to add to their already-overcrowded schedule. They were spared that option, though, when Kellett put them back in front with his second penalty and Holliday landed one of the long-dis-

Bill Holliday, who, with Frank Foster, was the subject of a sensational approach by Leeds which overshadowed the opening of new floodlights at Craven Park in September 1967.

Chris Davidson, who raced in for a try as Hull dramatically hit back at Craven Park in September 1967 in the first-ever BBC2 Floodlit Trophy derby.

tance drop goals that were to become one of his trademarks. It came near the end and finally sunk Hull 12-8.

It was be a little more than three years before Hull and Rovers met in another BBC2 Floodlit Trophy tie. Their second meeting in the competition took place in the second round at Craven Park on November 3, 1970, a little more than three months after Hull had knocked Rovers out of the Yorkshire Cup following two successive draws between the clubs earlier in the year. This time the gate was a mere 4,540, but there was one distinct comparison with that first derby meeting in the competition because Rovers were again involved in some busy transfer activity in the build-up. The day before the match Rovers announced that they were giving a trial to Featherstone Rovers' Great Britain Under-24 international prop Les Tonks with winger Greg

Ballantyne going to Post Office Road in exchange on trial. The Robins were also in the market for two Australian backs, Geoff Druery and Rod Jackson, while just before the match they agreed terms to sign Leeds' former York hooker Tony Crosby as a rival for the unsettled Peter Flanagan.

Hull were without Paul Ibbertson because of illness, so Nick Trotter deputised, while winger Alf Macklin was recalled. Rovers' trio of Gordon Young, Paul Rose and Brian Brook were all passed fit, but they had a big doubt about goalkicking prop Terry Clawson, an influential figure who was on the transfer list at £8,000 at the time. He had been struggling with a back injury, but in the end he decided to play, battled through the pain barrier and made a major impact on what turned out to be some stormy proceedings.

Statistically, it was quite simply the first Hull derby since 1902 in which as many as three players were sent off. Rovers' scrum-half Colin Cooper was the first to go when he paid the price for a 33rd-minute free-for-all; Flanagan was their second player to be dismissed when he aimed a punch at Chris Davidson as Hull's scrum-half tried to get the ball from him for a 54th-minute penalty; and six minutes later Davidson himself was sent for the traditional early bath after striking Paul Rose. But Clawson was to prove the difference between the sides because he kicked five goals out of five from awkward positions, while his oppo-

Terry Clawson battled through the pain barrier to make a major impact on the BBC2 Floodlit Trophy tie at Craven Park in November 1970.

site number, Hull prop Eric Broom, landed only one goal out of five. And yet Clawson admitted later: 'My back was giving me hell for the full 80 minutes. I should never have played.'

Even so, Clawson put the Robins into the driving seat with three penalties and Flanagan chipped in with a drop goal to make it 8-0 by half-time. The Airlie Birds hit back with a try by their hooker Alan McGlone and this time Broom added the goal. But Clawson added two difficult conversions after Rovers' backs Max Rooms and John Moore had both squeezed in for tries in the corner and when Clive Sullivan touched down for Hull, it was by then only a token consolation effort. Rovers were through with an 18-8 triumph.

Although no one knew it at the time, of course, Rovers had just established an unassailable 2-0 lead over Hull in derby games in the BBC2 Floodlit Trophy because they were to meet only once more in the competition – a little more than nine years later. But the Airlie Birds were to derive maximum solace from it because this was arguably the most important meeting of the three. It was, after all, in the final and it attracted a capacity crowd of 18,500 to the Boulevard on the night of December 18, 1979. It was to be the last-ever BBC2 Floodlit Trophy final and that gate aptly produced a competition record.

Hull had not lost to Rovers in the the previous six derby meetings and they had faced a difficult path to the final because they had entered the competition in the preliminary round in which they had beaten Halifax 8-1. They had then defeated Huddersfield 34-2, Leeds 16-9 and Leigh 9-6 on their way to the final, while Rovers had got there by overcoming Castleford 25-12, Keighley 41-15 and St Helen's 10-7. And it was to be the only major cup final derby not to be decided on neutral territory as Hull sought to win the trophy for the first time after going down in three semifinals and Rovers strove to land it for the second time in three years.

The Robins' injured player-coach Roger Millward caused a few raise eyebrows when he plumped for Ian Robinson, normally a centre, at full-back in place of Steve Leighton, who was missing because of a bruised hip, in preference to switching David Hall from standoff half and bringing in Steve Hartley. As

Steve Dennison showed an eye for an opening at the Boulevard in December 1979 in the last-ever BBC2 Floodlit Trophy Final which attracted a competition record attendance.

it was, Hartley did come on as a substitute for much-travelled second-row forward Geoff Clarkson, who was completing the set of having appeared in every one of rugby league's major cup finals. Hull gave a derby debut to full-back Paul Woods and their hopes were helped by the recovery of two injured players, winger Steve Dennison, who had had an eye problem, and second-row forward Keith Boxall, who had had bruised ribs, while Keith Tindall was preferred to Charlie Birdsall at prop and centre Graham Walters was on the substitutes' bench as Phil Coupland got the nod ahead of him, enabling him to play against his old club for the first time. Intriguingly, though, it was to be Dennison's eye for an opening that was to play a significant role in the proceedings.

Dennison opened the scoring after 24 minutes when he converted his own try after following up his own kick and it was still 5-0 to Hull at half-time. Two minutes after the interval Dennison was on hand for a second conversion after a burst by Woods had enabled him to send Graham Evans over under the posts. Rovers battled back and in the 69th minute Steve Hubbard touched down in the corner when he beat Dennison to a clever kick by Allan Agar. But four minutes later the Airlie Birds restored their 10-point cushion when substitute Charlie Birdsall charged over. It finished 13-3 as Hull picked up their first major trophy for 21 years, but it was to turn out to be the precursor of an even more meaningful derby final that season. And that would be an occasion when the whole of Hull was lit up.

Rovers' Brian Mennell is stopped by Hull's Eric Broom (left) and Joe Brown in April 1969.

Hull winger Alf Macklin is stopped by Rovers' David Wainwright in April 1971.

Rovers' half-back John Moore scores the only try of the derby at Easter 1972.

Rovers' loose-forward Phil Lowe (right) emerges from a muddy clash in an Easter derby in 1972.

Hull's Alf Macklin scores his side's only try in a derby in April 1973.

Boothferry Battles

BECAUSE the derbies between Hull FC and Hull Kingston Rovers have by their very nature been an intensely private matter between two factions separated by a river that flows through an industrial heartland a fair bit of its way, it would always seem a trifle unnatural for them ever to take place outside the city. Outsiders might always be intrigued enough to want to observe the proceedings, but might they ever truly appreciate and understand the real intensity felt by those brought up inside the city's environs? There is, therefore, a logical argument to suggest that if derbies were not played simply on a customary home-and-away basis, then there should be only one other venue that should be allowed to host one of the games – Boothferry Park, the home of Hull City AFC since the end of World War Two.

It is, of course, neutral territory and in its pomp it was able to provide much more spacious, comfortable surroundings than the Boulevard or Craven Park. As a result, it would be perfectly acceptable to play out a derby drama at Boothferry Park so that what belonged to Hull as a city stayed with Hull as a city on a practical basis. In the 1980s, therefore, it was seen as an ideal venue for some – not all, in fact – cup finals between Hull and Rovers. It is supremely quirky to remember, therefore, that a number of derbies had already taken place at Boothferry Park that were, by comparison, mere league matches. That was because the Robins decided in their infinite wisdom that it would be more beneficial for them to play their 'home' league games at Boothferry Park instead of at Craven Park. And it happened on a regular basis between 1953 and 1959. It was, furthermore, particularly ironic that Rovers should choose to play their home games against Hull at Boothferry Park because they are the East Hull team and they were going to a ground in West Hull to play their West Hull rivals. It is at such quaint times that it is considerably comforting to know that there really is no such place as South Hull to complicate matters further – it is the River Humber instead!

The first derby at Boothferry Park took place on April 3, 1953, and was a notable occasion all-round. The crowd of 27,670 paid record derby receipts of £3,280 and Widnes referee George Phillips broke a finger in a collision with Rovers forward Matt Anderson and had to relinquish control of the game for a time. In addition, there was a minute's silence before the game in memory of Rovers full-back Laurie Osborne, who had died earlier in the week. Hull were without half-back Bernard Conway because of a leg injury in a game that threw up two intriguing tussles in the forwards. Hull's Johnny Whiteley was opposing his England predecessor Alec Dockar at loose-forward and there were two top-class hookers on show, the Airlie

Birds' international Tommy Harris and the Robins' Sam Smith, who had just earned Yorkshire honours.

Hull's 'great pack' were beginning to burgeon and Whiteley held the aces on this occasion, scoring the first try, to which Colin Hutton added the conversion. There was then an action replay with Hutton tacking on the goal to Whiteley's second try before full-back Denis Chalkley reduced the arrears for Rovers with a penalty. Whiteley also set up Hull's third try, scored by winger Gerry Cox, as they ended up as 13-2 winners.

There was another derby at Boothferry Park later in the year and it was the first to be played in the city under floodlights. It took place on September 21, 1953, in front of a gate of 16,720 and there was also a new look to both sides. Hull gave a chance to winger Jim Staples, who had been signed from Boulevard Juniors at the start of the season, in what was to be his only derby appearance, while Rovers had four local derby debutants – 22-year-old winger Arthur Garry, who had been signed from Reckitt's 24 hours earlier, Terry Buckle, Ernest Knapp and Brian Beck. The Airlie Birds were without the injured Colin Hutton, Roy Francis and Johnny Whiteley, while Ivor Watts was away on county duty. The Robins were without Derek Turner and Tom Sutton, who had received a cheek injury against Huddersfield two days earlier, but player-coach Bryn Knowelden and prop Frank Moore returned to the side.

Buckle gave Rovers the lead with a sixth-minute penalty before loose-forward Arthur Bedford dashed in for

Hull's first try 15 minutes later. Harry Markham went on two blistering runs to add further tries for Hull, who had led 6-4 at the break after Buckle's second penalty. And the Airlie Birds' 15-4 victory was secured by three penalties from Carl Turner, but they paid a heavy price for their success. Markham, Staples, Bedford, Tommy Harris and Norman Hockley were all injury casualties although Rovers did not escape entirely because second-row forward Jim Tong was reduced to being a virtual passenger with an ankle injury.

Hull also won the third derby to be played at Boothferry Park when 17,155 fans saw a Good Friday clash on April 8, 1955. The Airlie Birds were without player-coach Roy Francis because of a gashed lip, so Derek Brindle was given another opportunity in the centre. The Robins gave derby debuts to backs Keith Goulding and Bernard Golder, the former Leicester rugby union winger, and welcomed back John Parker at scrum-half and Jim Tong at hooker, but they were without the injured Brian Beck and John Hall. Curiously, though, they omitted a trialist half-back because he was 'not considered sufficiently experienced' for such an encounter!

Hull, in fact, had to make a late change with Keith Bowman taking Stan Cowan's place on the wing and it proved to be a significant switch because he ran in two tries. Terry Buckle put Rovers in front with a penalty, but Bowman's tries, one more by Carl Turner and two penalties by Colin Hutton gave Hull the initiative. The Robins did not get on to the scoresheet again until the final minute when Tong and Frank Moore fashioned a try for Geoff Tullock, but Hull ran out 13-5 winners. The main casualties were Hull's Hutton, Tommy Harris and Bernard Conway, while Rovers' centre Pat Austin went off with a shoulder injury.

Rovers finally won a 'home' game at Boothferry Park later that year after they had suddenly clicked into gear with five wins from six matches. It took place on October 8, 1955, and the 16,670 crowd were treated to a thriller. Hull rested international prop Bob Coverdale, but welcomed Harry Markham back into their pack after a leg injury. Stand-off half Pat Austin failed a late fitness test for Rovers.

There was little to choose between the two sides early on when it was 4-4 with Sam Evans landing a penalty and John Parker dropping a goal for Rovers and Colin Hutton kicking two long-range penalties for Hull. But prop Ken Grice scored the first try of the game and Evans added the conversion to give Rovers a 9-4 lead at half-time. Evans then made it 11-4 with another penalty before Hull hit back dramatically to run in four tries from Bill Riches, Mick Scott, Rowley Moat and Ivor Watts. Hutton converted two of them to put the Airlie Birds 20-11 ahead, but then the Robins, in turn, showed their mettle to mount a comeback. Evans converted tries by Keith Goulding and Jim Shires, whose effort was hotly-disputed, to nudge them 21-20 ahead and that was how it stayed after Hutton had missed a late penalty chance to prevent one further dramatic twist to the proceedings.

Hull returned to winning away in West Hull in the next Boothferry Park

Stan Cowan, one of the try-scorers in the 1957 Boothferry Park derby game.

derby exactly 51 weeks later. There was a crowd of 18,742 for what was Leeds referee 'Sergeant-Major' Eric Clay's first derby appointment on October 1, 1956. Hull were at full strength, but Rovers were without their leading try-scorer Brian Shaw because of injury and his place on the wing went to teenager John Chapman, who had been signed from Boulevard Juniors, in preference to John Moore. They welcomed back captain Jim Tong, but Tom Sutton was missing from their pack.

Referee Clay made his mark just after half-time when he reduced Hull to 12 men by sending off Jim Drake for a trip on Rovers forward Dennis Johnson, but they made light of it and the difference between the two sides was the superior kicking of Colin Hutton. He kicked a penalty and then converted a well-worked try by scrum-half Tommy Finn, but after Rovers had twice gone close, they reduced the arrears with a try by John Hall following a scissors movement. Terry Buckle added the conversion to make it 7-5 at half-time, but Hutton kicked two more penalties before converting Mick Scott's last-minute try to give the Airlie Birds a 16-5 triumph.

There were some interesting selections in the teams for the next Boothferry Park derby a year later when 20,156 fans turned up for what was a one-sided game on October 7, 1957. Hull had Tommy Finn back at scrum-half in place of John Smith and Brian Saville resumed at centre with Geoff Dannatt switching to the wing instead of Keith Bowman, who was a surprise omission because he had scored a hat-trick tries in the previous game against Dewsbury. Ivor Watts was missing because of influenza and Colin Cole was ruled out by a thigh injury, but another surprise was the rare appearance of Colin Hutton, normally a full-back, in the second row at the expense of Peter Whiteley. Rovers, for their part, gave a derby debut to teenage winger George Garton, a former Charterhouse schoolboy soccer player, in place of Ernest Wilson, who had influenza. They were without injury victims Harold Ellerby and John Hall, but Sam Evans took his place in the forwards despite having suffered a torn ear in the recent clash with Doncaster and they decided not to risk student David Simpkin.

For the first time since Christmas Day, 1948, Rovers failed to score in a derby as Hull established a 15-point lead by half-time. Stan Cowan, Jim Drake and Tommy Finn ran in tries, which were supplemented by two conversions and a penalty by Peter Bateson. In the second half the Airlie Birds scored two more tries as Saville carried Brian Shaw over the line with him and Cowan went over in the corner to give them a 21-0 victory.

The next encounter at Boothferry Park between Hull and Rovers took place on Good Friday in front of 21,594 fans on March 27, 1959 – just six days after another derby. Hull had just beaten Rovers 23-9 in the third round of the Rugby League Challenge Cup and they were to make sure that revenge was not in the air. The brief build-up surrounded the respective full-backs, Hull's Peter Bateson and Rovers' Cyril Kellett. Bateson, the former Batley player, had discussed his future at the Boulevard with the directors because Arthur Keegan had displaced him and he had not had a regular first-team place since recovering from injury. The prolific Kellett, meanwhile, was just two points short of scoring 200 points in a season for the first time after already clocking up 93 goals and four tries. His teammate Brian Coulson, furthermore, was closing in on Rovers' try-scoring record of 26 in a season by Geoff Tullock after scoring in five successive games and was five short of his target. But the Robins, who also brought Jack Rogers and John Keegan into their pack, were without Ken Grice and Alvin Ackerley and had a problem at scrum-half because of injuries to David Elliott and Peter Key. As it was, Key passed a late fitness test.

The high-scoring game did enable Kellett to achieve his target – Coulson moved no nearer his – but Bateson played an even more important role in the proceedings. He landed a conversion after Johnny Whiteley had followed up Ivor Watts' kick for the first try. Stan Cowan touched down for the second before Kellett reached 200 points for the season with a conversion after Key had sold a dummy to George Garton to go over and make it 8-5. Rovers claimed in vain that Cowan and Whiteley had both failed to get over the line for their second tries and Cowan increased Hull's lead before Kellett landed two penalties to to leave it 13-9 at the break. Bateson had already kicked a further goal and he then landed three penalties before Graham Paul raced in at the corner to cut Rovers' deficit to 19-12. But Whiteley's controversial try, which Bateson converted for his sixth goal, completed the scoring as Hull won 24-12.

At that point the Football Association banned rugby league from their grounds – a remarkable decision to contemplate nowadays in view of the constant talks about ground-sharing between different sports – so Rovers returned to Craven Park for their home derbies. In view of their poor record at Boothferry Park, they probably classified the FA's intervention as timely.

And it was more than 25 years before Hull and Rovers returned to Boothferry Park when it was chosen as the logical venue for a Yorkshire Cup final between them both on October 27, 1984. Hull had beaten Halifax at home, York away

and Leeds at home on their way to the final as they strove to win the trophy for the third consecutive season. And everything looked strangely ominous when groundsman Stan Coombs and his assistant Frank Mobbs found a full team of miniature garden gnomes dressed in Hull's colours on their hallowed Boothferry Park turf just hours before the start with one accompanying Rovers gnome lying on his side nearby with his head snapped off! Hull, though, were without their international prop Trevor Skerrett because of knee trouble and Paul Rose was only on the substitutes' bench after a hamstring problem. But Gary Divorty returned at loose-forward after a four-match absence with a hamstring injury and winger James Leuluai had recovered from a neck problem, while Fred Ah Kuoi was preferred to David Topliss at stand-off half. Rovers were without injured scrum-half Gordon Smith, but centre Gary Prohm and loose-forward David Hall passed late fitness checks, while Ian Robinson returned in the backs.

It was not quite a game of two very different halves, but the scoring was divided into two parts. Rovers scored first and then Hull scored more points second! The Robins were 12-0 ahead after 30 minutes following tries by Robinson, George Fairbairn and Hall, but after Garry Schofield had reduced the arrears with a penalty, he converted a try by Hull's 21-year-old captain Lee Crooks to leave it more delicately poised at 12-8 by half-time. The Airlie Birds then took a second-half stranglehold: having scored a minute before the break, they then scored again a minute after it when Gary Kemble touched down, Schofield added the touchline conversion and they took the lead for the first time at 14-12. Schofield dropped a goal ten minutes later and Kemble's second try on the hour should not have been a surprise because he was suffering from double vision! Steve Norton grabbed Hull's fourth try ten minutes from time, Schofield tacked on the conversion and Steve Evans completed the scoring by racing 80 yards for an interception try. Hull's only major setback was that amid it all Rose was dismissed for a high tackle only a minute after coming on as a 70th-minute substitute, but they had still gone from 12 points down to 29-12 winners and Rovers' Kiwi prop Mark Broadhurst acknowledged magnanimously: "To come from 12-0 down to win by 17 points has got to be one of the finest cup final recovery acts of all time."

To add further spice to a memorable season, however, the two clubs were back at Boothferry Park three months later for another cup final. This time it was in the John Player Trophy and the attendance was a little better because 25,326 spectators, who brought in receipts of £69,555, saw Rovers gain their revenge on January 26, 1985. But a volunteer force, including some of Hull City's youngsters, had to work hard to make sure that the pitch was fit for play after a blizzard less than 48 hours before the game. Hull had Lee Crooks back in their pack after a fractured cheekbone, while Dane O'Hara and Peter Sterling recovered from groin strains to play and prop Phil Edmonds passed a fitness test on a damaged ankle, but three other forwards, Trevor Skerrett, John Muggleton and Steve

Steve Evans, who raced 80 yards for an interception try in the 1984 Yorkshire Cup final at Boothferry Park.

Norton, were ruled out by injuries. Rovers, who had signed Gary Sims and Bruce Miller during the build-up, were without forward Andy Kelly because of a damaged ankle and his place went to Phil Hogan, but prop Asuquo 'Zook' Ema was able to play after recovering from a knee injury.

There was one stark statistic to emerge from the clash as Rovers won the trophy for the first time because Hull, eventually so free-scoring three months earlier, failed to score in a derby clash for the first time since Christmas Day, 1965. Even more simply, the Robins scored three tries again as they opened the scoring, but did not permit the Airlie Birds to reply at all as they marched to a rare vic-

Paul Harkin won successive man-of-the-match awards in the John Player Trophy final in the mid-1980s.

tory at Boothferry Park. Gary Prohm forced his way over for the first try after 13 minutes and four minutes later Hogan took Gavin Miller's pass to add a second. Eight minutes from the end winger Garry Clark completed the scoring when he went in at the corner and Paul Rose escaped with just a booking on this occasion, later admitting in true derby spirit: 'Someone hit me first. I do not hit anybody unless they start it!' Rovers' scrum-half Paul Harkin took the man-of-the-match award – a feat that he repeated the following season – and Hull drowned their sorrows by jetting off for a four-day break in Majorca.

The next derby at Boothferry Park took place on August 10, 1997, in front of

a crowd of just 7,500 after rugby league had been switched to the summer. Another change was to the regime at Boothferry Park because Tim Wilby, once Hull's try-scorer against Rovers at Wembley, was just completing a takeover for Hull City in conjunction with tennis supremo David Lloyd, who was Great Britain's non-playing Davis Cup captain at the time. It was to lead to Wilby becoming chairman of both Hull and the Tigers for a brief period before he moved to Australia and Lloyd took a firmer grip on matters in his own forthright fashion. Significantly in derby history it was to be the only game at Boothferry Park to be a home fixture for Hull and it occurred when controversial proposals to move City to the Boulevard for ground-sharing were first being mooted. Hull, by

Tim Wilby in his playing days. Once a try scorer for Hull at Wembley, he took over at Boothferry Park in conjuction with David Lloyd in 1997.

Mike Fletcher came on as a substitute at Boothferry Park in 1997 and emerged a hero.

now known as the Sharks to the detriment of many years' tradition, welcomed back prop Andy Dannatt, sent off in a derby clash two months earlier, in place of Alex Thompson, whose loan spell from Sheffield Eagles had ended. Leading points-scorer Mark Hewitt returned at scrum-half, but full-back Steve Holmes was missing because of an ankle problem, so former Rovers player Graeme Hallas replaced him. Forwards

Brad Hepi and David Boyd were on the substitutes' bench after having been doubtful because of injuries. Rovers' Mike Fletcher was back on the substitutes' bench after recovering from a broken collarbone with Bob Everitt keeping his place at full-back.

Mike Fletcher did get his chance to join the proceedings after 51 minutes when he took over from Darren Hutchinson and he was to emerge as Rovers' hero with a memorable comeback because he outjumped Hull's winger Mark Johnson to reach a kick from his skipper Wayne Parker and score the match-winning try in the final minute. Johnson, in fact, had opened the scoring with the first try, which Hewitt converted after just 90 seconds, so the start was as dramatic as the finish. Rovers winger Paul Rouse touched down after 13 minutes, but Hewitt landed two penalties to make it 10-4. Centre Tevita Vaikona crossed for Hull's second try, Hewitt landed a touchline conversion and they were 16-4 in front by the interval. Two minutes into the second half Paul Fletcher scored Rovers' second try and Everitt added the conversion, but Hull restored their 12-point advantage when Hewitt converted Vaikona's second try. Everitt made it 22-12 with a penalty and converted a 72nd-minute try by centre Garry Atkins as the Robins' comeback gained momentum. Everitt kicked another penalty and then Mike Fletcher became the toast of East Hull as Rovers, whose squad comprised 13 local players, sneaked home 24-22.

Hull's Steve Norton challenges Rovers' Len Casey in a 1982 derby.

Rovers' Garry Clark touches down in April 1984.

Rovers' coach Roger Millward looks on from the dug-out in a 1991 derby.

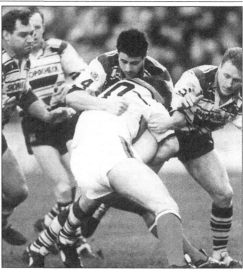

A tough clash during a New Year derby in 1992.

Crunching action from a derby in April 1992.

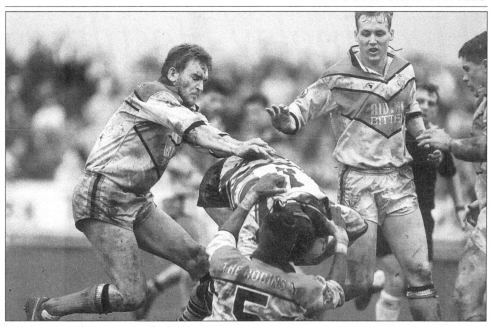

Hectic action from a 1992 derby.

A fierce contest in a derby during the 1992-93 season.

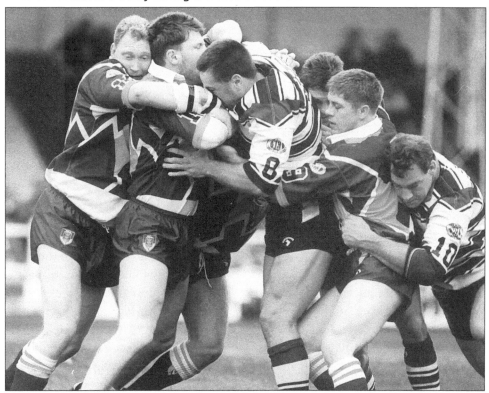

Headingley Hostilities

ALTHOUGH Boothferry Park has been selected to host cup finals between Hull FC and Hull Kingston Rovers, there is one other neutral ground which has opened up its doors to the rival factions on even more occasions – Headingley. It may appear to be incongruous and illogical for the followers of the two clubs to be compelled to traipse all the way across Yorkshire to Leeds to watch a derby game, but it has happened. And no one has really batted an eyelid in the face of such an unkind and awkward consideration, bearing in mind that the earliest of such cup final clashes took place before the M62 was available to speed up and facilitate the journey. The fans' philosophy was probably that if you had to leave Hull to travel to West Yorkshire to watch a derby spectacle, then you had much more scope and time to make the most of the journey home when you had won. And the other possibility was never worth much serious conjecture because defeat, after all, would never be openly contemplated beforehand even though one of the two factions would have to contend with it. And the losers might, of course, find it distinctly handy to remain in West Yorkshire for a while in the immediate aftermath to drown their sorrows rather than to return straightaway to a fiercely-divided city to have to endure the awful consequences.

Travel was certainly difficult on the first trip to north-west Leeds for a derby between Hull and Rovers in the Yorkshire Cup final on November 27, 1920. It was the first time that the two clubs had met in a final and meant that the Yorkshire Cup, inaugurated in 1905, ten years after the formation of the Northern Union, would at least come to the East Riding for the first time. Hull had reached the final with an 18-5 win at Keighley and a 31-5 success at home to Hunslet, while Rovers had taken a slightly longer route via victories over Bradford Northern 12-3, Leeds 8-2 away and Dewsbury 8-5. The fact that Hull and Rovers were both near the top of the league table added extra edge to a clash that attracted a crowd of about 20,000.

It did not take long for the atmosphere of the occasion to come to the fore on the morning of the match as the great exodus began. It was reported: 'Thousands of visitors to the Yorkshire Cup final left Paragon Station during the morning. The ordinary trains were crowded to their utmost capacity and four extra ones were run. Supporters of both the rivals arrived at the station in a steady flow and took their seats in the trains with little ado. Many of them displayed the colours of their respective sides and here and there on the carriages were chalk drawings of the trophy with 'Hull' or 'Rovers' written across them. Among the passengers were a number of ladies and not a few boys.

'The first of the special trains went

out on the stroke of 11 o'clock, conveying more than 1,000 passengers. About 4,000 passengers left from Paragon Station for Leeds by the four special trains and two ordinary trains during the morning. The teams left at 11.47am by a special train. Rovers arrived at the station first and the players, directors and supporters were accommodated in the fore part of the train. They were closely followed by the Hull team and officials, who were also accompanied by a number of supporters. The train moved out with no outward indication that it conveyed the men who were to take part in the great struggle for the Yorkshire Northern Union Cup.

'Four trains also left Cannon Street station during the morning and all were packed. They left at about 11.10am, 11.25am, 11.35am and 11.50am and in all it was calculated by the stationmaster that about 2,700 travelled on them. In many instances extra coaches had to be obtained and even then there was little or no room for late arrivals. On boards were chalked up the names of those who had booked saloons, including Peel House Club, the Tally Ho! Hotel, East Hull Working Men's Club, East Hull Conservatives, Kingston Bowling Club and various hotels and recreation clubs. Some people had their spirits slightly dampened by the downpour of rain, but the general feeling was one of enthusiasm. Enterprising hawkers were on the scene at an early hour, disposing of their black-and-white and red-and-white at a brisk rate. Wearers of the colours indulged in good-natured chaff.'

Rovers went into the game as the underdogs simply because they had not beaten Hull in 12 successive peacetime games dating back to Boxing Day, 1913. The closest they had come in that spell was an 8-8 draw in September 1919. And it was very much a local occasion on the pitch because 14 of the players were from Hull and district rugby – ten in Rovers' team and four in Hull's side. But it was scarcely an open game and after Hull's former Barrow forward Bob Taylor had had a 'try' disallowed, all the signs indicated a pointless draw until there was a dramatic finale conjured up by one of the outsiders, Billy Bradshaw, the Robins' winger from Northampton. Rovers' pack had dominated much of the game with their hooker Sandy Gibson winning the scrums by about a two-to-one margin, but the vital breakthrough did not come until three minutes from the end. Bradshaw fielded a clearing kick from Hull's full-back Ned Rogers, took careful aim and dropped a sensational goal to win the cup. And it was claimed: 'That goal will be talked about as long as rugby football is played in Hull. It was no fluke, but an act of wonderful judgment and deliberation because it was the only alternative to a drawn game. The ending was as sensational as it was unexpected, but, taking everything into consideration, it was eminently satisfactory. No one wanted to see a drawn game because the excitement had been all-sufficient for one week.' There was a civic reception to follow at Hull City Hall and it was Rovers' captain Arthur Moore who held the Yorkshire Cup aloft after a 2-0 triumph.

If that were not enough, there was to be a second trip to Headingley for a derby clash later that season. Rovers topped the league, then decided on a percentage basis, at the end of the season on 76.56 with Hull in second place on 75. The top four qualified for the championship play-offs with Hull beating Halifax 27-10 and Rovers defeating Wigan 26-4 in the semi-finals. It meant that the old rivals squared up to each other again in the final on May 7, 1921, and history remarkably repeated itself because there were just two points between the two sides once more.

This time, though, the travelling arrangements were different. Rovers went by train from Paragon Station at 8.08am and then used the White Horse restaurant in Leeds as their pre-match headquarters. But Hull's players and officials journeyed by motor charabancs, leaving the Imperial Hotel in the city's Paragon Street at 9am, stopping for dinner at Selby en route. There was not the same travelling support from Hull as there had been for the Yorkshire Cup final, though, and the game attracted an attendance of only 10,000 on this occasion. Luckily the Leeds tramway service had been restored for the event to ease congestion in the city, but fans of both sides ended up in Selby on the way home and the train journey from Leeds lasted five hours!

Hull were without the injured Alf Francis, but both teams were otherwise at full strength after several injury scares and both were seeking to complete a double. Hull were the league cup holders after winning the championship play-offs final the previous season and Rovers, of course, were the Yorkshire Cup holders.

Hull set out to avenge that Yorkshire Cup final defeat in determined fashion, leading 9-4 at half-time and 14-4 soon afterwards, but in the final 20 minutes Rovers mounted a rally in which they closed the deficit from ten points to two at one stage. Sandy Gibson, though, missed a comfortable-looking conversion in the last minute and the Robins' chance of a draw had gone. At the same time Hull centre Jim Kennedy had seen a first-half conversion strike an upright when they scored tries through Billy Stone, Jimmy Devereux and Bob Taylor, who touched down again in the second half. Rovers managed two goals from Gibson in the first half and he added a further two after the interval when they also managed tries from Cook and Mulvey. Kennedy landed two second-half goals and Hull were home and dry by a 16-14 margin.

As fate would have it, the two clubs did not go back to Headingley to meet each other again until October 14, 1967. Little had changed in the interim, though, because the game was again a very close affair and the Yorkshire Cup was at stake once more. The final attracted a gate of 16,734 and only one point separated the two sides on this occasion. By this time Rovers, who were defending an unbeaten 13-match run, were the Yorkshire Cup holders and Hull had won only once in 12 finals in the competition. The Airlie Birds had beaten Castleford 13-7, Halifax 11-2 and Leeds 31-6 at home on their way to the final, while the Robins had overcome York 22-4, Wakefield Trinity 14-5 in a replay after a 13-13-draw and Dewsbury 21-0 en route. Hull were without forward Jim Neale, who had damaged his thumb in

Alan Burwell scored the match-winning try at Headingley in the 1967 Yorkshire Cup final.

ination. As it was, Hull took the intiative with a try by Davidson after just three minutes before Roger Millward pulled off an interception to go over for the Robins. Hull's John Maloney and Rovers' Cyril Kellett exchanged penalties and it was 5-5 at half-time. But Davidson, the winner of the White Rose trophy for the man of the match, dropped a 58th-minute goal to edge the Airlie Birds back in front only for their hearts to be broken towards the end when Rovers winger Alan Burwell took Terry Major's pass and went over in the corner for the match-winning try. The trophy went to Rovers' acting captain John Moore after an 8-7 triumph.

The next derby final at Headingley was in the Premiership play-offs on May 16, 1981, and attracted a crowd of 30,000 to what was a rugby league showpiece. And it was fitting that the referee, John Holdsworth, was from Leeds. Hull had finished seventh in the First Division and had beaten Warrington 19-7 and then Castleford 12-11 on their way to the final, while Rovers had defeated Widnes 14-12 and St Helen's 30-17 after ending up third in the table. The Airlie Birds' preparations were hampered by a shock transfer request from scrum-half Clive Pickerill three days before the match and he annoyed team manager Arthur Bunting by insisting that he would rather work than play in any case. Tony Dean took his place, but the additional possibility of 'Sammy' Lloyd making a dramatic return to the line-up did not materialise, while Graham Walters was suspended and Graham Bray was injured, so teenager David Elliott played only his second senior game for the club.

the semi-final victory over Leeds, but Cyril Sykes had recovered from influenza and Alan McGlone and Chris Davidson had shrugged off knocks. Rovers were at full strength and opted to leave their rugged forward Frank Foster on the substitutes' bench after a long absence with a damaged hand.

A blustery wind and showery rain marred the proceedings and Hull indulged in some spoiling tactics to try to frustrate Rovers. They succeeded for long periods until the introduction of Foster gave the Robins a little more dom-

Rovers' skipper Len Casey celebrates after his side had won the Premiership final at Headingley in May 1981.

Rovers were without long-term absentees Paul Rose, Steve Crooks and Ian Robinson for what was their third final of the season, but their international hooker David Watkinson was passed fit to play.

Rovers made their extra pace pay dividends to run in three tries to Hull's one and had taken control of the game by half-time when they were 8-2 ahead. Phil Hogan scored the Robins' first try, to which Steve Hubbard added a touchline conversion, and Steve Hartley raced 65 yards for the second before Hull reduced the arrears with a 38th-minute penalty by full-back Paul Woods, who had struck the woodwork with a previous attempt. Mike Smith, who later had a brief coaching spell at the Boulevard, was Rovers' third try-scorer when he went over early in the second half. Mick Crane scored a 63rd-minute try for the Airlie Birds and Woods kicked another goal to keep things interesting to the end, but Rovers won the trophy for the first time with an 11-7 success. The Robins' skipper Len Casey won the Harry Sunderland Trophy for the man of the match against his old club, while defeat provided a sad finale for Charles Watson, who had decided to step down as Hull's chairman. But amid the mixed emotions there was already talk of transfer activity in both camps because the Robins were linked with a move for Great Britain captain George Fairbairn, who had been sacked as Wigan's coach the previous month, while Hull director and former centre Dick Gemmell was getting ready to jet off to New Zealand in an attempt to sign Test stars James Leuluai and Dane O'Hara.

Within a year Hull and Rovers were back at Headingley for another final. This time it was in the John Player Trophy and it was on January 23, 1982, in front of 25,245 fans. It came just 20 days after Hull had beaten Rovers 11-1 in the league at the Boulevard and both games were refereed by Wakefield's Fred Lindop, who had taken charge of the 1980 Wembley final between the two clubs. Hull had not been at home on their way to the final, having won 26-7 at Halifax, 23-5 at Castleford, Barrow 14-12 and 22-6 against Oldham in the semi-finals. Rovers had won 34-2 at Dewsbury, defeated Featherstone Rovers 18-6 at home and sneaked home 9-8 at Widnes before knocking out

Ronnie Wileman, who ran half the length of the Headingley pitch to score a try in the 1982 John Player Trophy final.

Swinton 23-14 in the semi-finals, both of which had also been at Headingley. Hull were without Kiwi full-back Gary Kemble because of an ankle injury and Tony Dean was preferred to Kevin Harkin at scrum-half, while Rovers included winger Steve Hubbard, who had just recovered from a minor knee operation.

Rovers did have an injury setback during the match, though, when scrum-half Paul Harkin had to be replaced by Chris Burton after half an hour. And just before he finally limped off, Hull took advantage with a simple penalty by teenager Lee Crooks and a try by hooker Ron Wileman after he had dashed half the length of the pitch. George Fairbairn cut the arrears to 5-2 by half-time with a 35th-minute penalty for Rovers, but Dean dropped a goal, which flew over off the post, to edge Hull further ahead after 49 minutes and then Crooks landed three more penalties to one more by Fairbairn. The Airlie Birds won 12-4, but there was a sour note five minutes from time when their captain 'Charlie' Stone was sent off for butting Mike Smith and Rovers' Roy Holdstock was also dismissed following his reaction to the incident.

Wembley Way

ON THE afternoon of May 3, 1980, a total of 3,297 fans watched professional sport in Hull. That was the attendance at Boothferry Park as Hull City tried to stave off what was then Fourth Division soccer for the first time in their history. They did so with a 1-0 win over Southend United, but it was very much the sub-plot in one of the most remarkable and memorable days in Hull's sporting history. The fact that there were even 3,297 fans at Boothferry Park was amazing in itself. The fact that anyone was left in Hull that day at all is equally so. Urban legend has it that somewhere on the western outskirts of the city that weekend there was a sign which wrily asked: 'Will the last one out please turn off the lights?'

The reason behind it all was simply that it was the day on which Hull's wildest rugby league dream became reality. That main plot was that the afternoon's Rugby League Challenge Cup final at Wembley was a largely private affair because it took place between Hull FC and Hull Kingston Rovers and outsiders had no sensitive or sensible part to play in the drama because they really could not understand what it meant to the city. There is a parallel in the legendary cricket story of a Roses match between Yorkshire and Lancashire when a southerner strangely joined the spectators. When a Lancashire batsman hit a boundary, the southerner is supposed to

have muttered: "Well played, sir." At this point a suspicious Yorkshire follower is said to have asked the southerner about his background and then, when given an honest answer, told him to shut up because the game was really none of his business! The same kind of philosophy probably applied that day at Wembley. It was the city of Hull's day out, it was the city of Hull's big sporting occasion and outsiders with views or passing interest either way were really interfering busybodies who were out of their depth in trying valiantly, but hopelessly to place the game into its most meaningful context.

That background had already included one derby cup final during the 1979-80 season and three other meetings. Hull won 27-20 in the final Eva Hardaker Memorial Trophy game and then there was a 20-20 draw when the sides again met at the Boulevard in the league. The Airlie Birds won 13-3 in the last BBC2 Floodlit Trophy final in December 1979, but a month before the Wembley date Rovers triumphed in the return league game 29-14 at Craven Park to end a run of eight derbies without a win.

Hull's Rugby League Challenge Cup campaign had started with a 33-10 won over amateur side Millom at the Boulevard and an 18-8 home victory over York. They nudged past Bradford Northern 3-0 at Odsal and then beat Widnes 10-5 – an ominous scoreline – at

A sea of fans mark the 1980 Wembley final.

Swinton in the semi-finals. Rovers won 18-3 at Wigan and then had two home victories – 28-3 over Castleford and 23-11 over Warrington – before beating Halifax 20-7 at Headingley in the their semi-final.

The build-up had been fascinating, though, because the possibility of a derby date at Wembley emerged once the sides had been kept apart in the semi-final draw. Rovers reached Wembley first with the win over Halifax, so what did their fans now want? Did they want Hull to fall at their semi-final hurdle or did they actually want them to get through – in other words, support them for a day in direct opposition to their basic beliefs – so that the ultimate derby could ensue? The followers of rugby league in Hull have always been a close-knit fraternity who have respected their chosen code and wanted it to be popular and success-

ful and the thought of a Wembley derby was probably too good to miss. Probably most Rovers fans spent the time between the two semi-finals thinking that it would nice for the code in the city over-all if Hull also reached Wembley, but there had to be a proviso that they were beaten once they got there! As it was, Hull just sneaked through in the closing stages of a dramatic semi-final against Widnes and the city's rugby league aficionados, like Martin Luther King before them in a totally different context, had a dream.

As rugby league fever took a strangle-hold, the players with both clubs were naturally anxious to be part of the Wembley proceedings, but there had to be disappointments. Hull's centre Graham Evans, a candidate for a place on the substitutes' bench, pulled a muscle in what should have been an innocuous

The all-Hull invasion of Wembley.

game of five-a-side soccer 48 hours before the final and missed out, while club captain Vince Farrar was omitted from the starting-line-up by manager Arthur Bunting. He did at least get a place on the substitutes' bench. Mick Crane and Paul Harkin were left out by Rovers' player-coach Roger Millward when he finalised his line-up after second-row forward Phil Lowe had passed a fitness on a damaged shoulder.

The game itself was watched by what was then a capacity crowd of 95,000, who paid receipts of £447,000. It was

Fans on the march to Wembley.

Hull players set off for Wembley.

estimated that there were between 25,000 and 30,000 fans from the city of Hull, most of whom invaded London on 28 special trains or 42 coaches. One Hull car-hire firm trebled their business and had to bring in ten transporter loads of extra vehicles to cope with the demand. The first fans entered Wembley shortly after 2pm for a game which was watched by the Queen Mother.

In true derby tradition the match had its moments of drama and controversy and was a low-scoring affair. Rovers opened the scoring after eight minutes when Brian Lockwood set up a try for winger Steve Hubbard, who later admitted with a splendid touch of irony: 'It was a planned move based on an idea that Brian Lockwood had brought over from Australia and we'd worked on it on the training ground, but we tried it about half-a-dozen times and I dropped the ball every time. I couldn't get the timing right because it involved a split-second move, but on the day we decided we'd have a go and the rest is history.' But there was a foul on Hubbard by a combination of Paul Woods and Graham Bray after he had scored, so he was able to increase the Robins' lead with a penalty after failing with the conversion. In the meantime, Millward had his jaw broken by a stiff-arm tackle from Hull's hooker Ron Wileman and then 'Charlie' Stone was penalised soon afterwards to give Hubbard the chance of a second penalty. It was Hubbard 7, Hull 0 after just a quarter of an hour.

Clive Pickerill and John Newlove finally got the Airlie Birds' scoring under

Rovers players in happy mood before the final.

Roger Millward is introduced to the Queen Mother.

The Queen Mother meets the Hull team.

Rival chairmen Rovers' Bill Land (left) and Hull's Charles Watson lead out the teams at Wembley in 1980.

way when they sent in centre Tim Wilby for a 28th-minute try, but 'Sammy' Lloyd missed the conversion on an afternoon when his normally-reliable kicking generally let him down. Three times the ball toppled over as he prepared for the conversion and in all he failed to land four out of five kicks. And as half-time approached, Millward nudged Rovers further ahead with a 30-yard, left-footed drop goal to make it 8-3 at the interval.

The Airlie Birds exerted plenty of pressure early in the second half and nine minutes after the resumption Bray had a 'try' disallowed when Lloyd was ruled to have obstructed David Hall. Three times during the afternoon Hull had 'tries' disallowed, but their chance of getting back into the game had gone even though Lloyd finally landed a 35-yard penalty to make it 8-5 after 51 minutes.

But nine minutes from time Hubbard kicked his third penalty although that was not the end of the drama for him. The score stayed 10-5 to the Robins, but Hubbard did not stay on the pitch throughout because he was replaced by Phil Hogan a minute from the end when he was carried off on a stretcher with a damaged ankle. He had scored nine of his side's ten points and mused later of the effect that his 40-yard dash to the try-line, in particular, had had on his home city's sporting history. He said: "I still get reminded about it and people have called me everything from a pig to a dog for scoring it. I've been on to building sites through work where people have thrown bricks at me although I think they've meant it as a joke. I think that try made an awful lot of people

Try-scorer Steve Hubbard is stretchered off with an ankle injury after notching nine of his team's ten points.

happy and an awful lot of people sad. It was one of the biggest highlights or low spots for Rovers and Hull supporters depending on which side they were on."

Brian Lockwood, the 1980 Lance Todd Trophy winner.

Previous page: **Clive Sullivan holds the RL Challenge Cup aloft.**

Oddly enough, he later played water-polo for Hull in the same team as Keith Tindall, who had been in the Airlie Birds' pack that day.

The derby atmosphere at such a major venue on such a big occasion naturally brought many mixed emotions in the two camps. Brian Lockwood, Millward's cousin who had joined Rovers after a spell as Wakefield Trinity's player-coach, won the Lance Todd Trophy for the man-of-the-match. And he reflected: "I got it for one pass to set up our match-winning try for Steve Hubbard, but I never thought that I had a particularly good game. But one thing that sticks in my memory about the Wembley triumph was that I had told Len Casey that it was the finest thing that could happen to a player, but he reckoned that the highspot was being in a touring party. We were on the top of the bus going down Holderness Road with the cup after getting back home when he turned and told me: 'You were right. Winning at Wembley is better than going to Australia.' I'd forgotten that I'd said it, but Len obviously hadn't."

In contrast, 'Sammy' Lloyd was devastated by his off-day when it mattered most to him. He recalled ruefully: "This was the biggest day of my life and I fluffed it. Just think of all those people who have come to expect me to kick goals. I let them down. I failed them. I thought it might be better if I moved." In fact, Lloyd stayed in the city as a popular publican and he added: "I was terrified of what reaction would come from the fans on our tour round Hull and back to the Boulevard. I expected them to jeer and boo me, but the reaction that I and the rest of the lads got was truly unbelievable. I just couldn't believe my ears as the fans continued to sing out those chants and songs even though we'd been beaten. It was a tonic I badly needed and it is something I'll never forget."

And the drama had not ended because there was an aftermath involving the coaches of both camps. Hull's team manager Arthur Bunting announced his resignation for business reasons soon afterwards although almost immediately

Geoff 'Sammy' Lloyd, whose normally reliable kicking let him down in the pressure-cooker atmosphere of a Wembley final.

he was persuaded to stay on after a special board meeting had been hastily convened and he signed a new three-year contract. Rovers' player-coach Roger Millward, then 32, wanted a new contract and he announced that he was seeking a five-year deal. In the end he also signed a new three-year contract.

Amid all the repercussions, there was a civic reception for both clubs at Hull Guildhall and it was an evening steeped in pride because the city's deputy Lord Mayor, Coun. Alex Clarke, declared: "It is an honour to pay tribute to the game and its supporters for their behaviour at Wembley. More than 60,000 people from the city of Hull were at Wembley and they provided not one moment of trou-

Rival fans assemble at Hull's Paragon Station in 1980.

ble for either the stadium officials or the police." And Rugby League secretary Sumner Baxendale added: "This was a unique occasion and, from a spectator point of view, this was a great Wembley and a credit to Hull FC and Hull KR. I have seen many Wembley finals, but this was the greatest of them all. The supporters were simply magnificent. You cannot praise the Hull people too highly."

And Rovers' scrum-half Allan Agar, Brian Lockwood's own nomination for the Lance Todd Trophy, put the players' perspective when he said: "My abiding memory is of the camaraderie between the two sets of fans. There is such intense rivalry between them in the city, but they created such a tremendous atmosphere on such a special day and that remains with me. In fact, the spectators made it into a greater occasion than the game itself deserved." And local rugby league all-time great Johnny Whiteley reflected: "I think that the city earned the game because there is such enthusiasm for rugby in Hull. I was proud because we again proved to the country what a sporting city we are. We got rave notices from everybody concerned with the sport. I have always waved a flag for Hull and been proud of the city and the Wembley final just put everything into perspective. Everyone was the winner." That, presumably, is known as building bridges across the river.

It had been arguably been the mother, father and Great Uncle Bulgaria of all derbies and a day to savour in the city of Hull's sporting heritage! It was the day on which all Hull broke loose in rugby league terms. Rovers fans probably felt that victory had proved something substantial once and for all when it really, really mattered and could claim that all ensuing derbies were inconsequential in

Rovers' players parade around Hull with the RL Challenge Cup in 1980.

Roger Millward shows off the RL Challenge Cup on Rovers' triumphant return home.

Roger Millward with the RL Challenge Cup.

comparison. Hull fans probably considered the result to be a clerical error and felt that it was just another game played for just another 80 minutes under just the customary conditions. To them it might be defined as one more derby in a never-ending saga of them and the importance of the venue was not a factor in the great scheme of the series. In reality, it had everything that 100 years of derbies between Hull FC and Hull Kingston Rovers had always produced. The difference was that on this occasion a city's sporting passion, built around a traditional rivalry that was nurtured by the natural divide provided by the river flowing through its heart, had reached a far wider stage.

ND - #0218 - 270225 - C0 - 234/156/7 - PB - 9781780914640 - Gloss Lamination